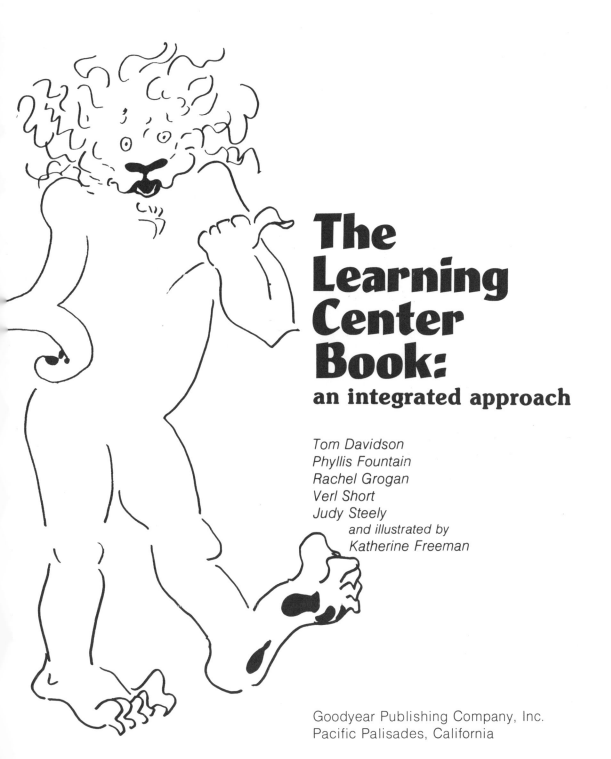

The Learning Center Book:
an integrated approach

Tom Davidson
Phyllis Fountain
Rachel Grogan
Verl Short
Judy Steely
 and illustrated by
 Katherine Freeman

Goodyear Publishing Company, Inc.
Pacific Palisades, California

Library of Congress Cataloging in Publication Data

Main entry under title:
The Learning Center Book . . .
    (Goodyear education series)
    Bibliography: p.
    1. Open plan schools. I. Davidson, Tom,
1941—II. Title.
LB1029.06L42   372.1'3   74-33858
ISBN 0-87620-528-7

Current Printing (last digit):
10 9 8 7 6 5 4 3 2 1

ISBN: 0-87620-530-9 (C)
ISBN: 0-87620-528-7 (P)

Y-5309-3 (C)
Y-5287-1 (P)

Cover and interior design: Linda Sanford Higgins
Supervising editor: Sue MacLaurin

Printed in the United States of America

To the many students and teachers
who are trying
to make learning meaningful,
without whom this book
would not exist,
and to children everywhere,
without whom the need for this book
would not exist.

preface

This publication has been fun to produce,
as it brought six of us together to
share ideas about schools, children, and
learning and helped us to know each other
as people as well as professionals.
We believe that this is a vitally important
part of education and teaching and
are proud we achieved some measure
of success as we worked on this project.

It was our desire to publish something
that could be used as a guide by
classroom practitioners in utilizing the
learning-center concept in developing a
better learning environment for individual
children. However, we hope that our
approach to centers—integration of
curriculum—will foster a broader
understanding of how children can
be aided in beginning to view learning as
an applicative endeavor rather than as an
effort to master isolated skills and facts
from isolated subject-matter domains.

All the centers in this book have been
field tested by preservice and inservice
teachers at West Georgia College
in Carrollton, Georgia and have been found
to be effective. The centers are
presented here as they were used in
classrooms with children. However, the
greatest use they may be to you will
probably be as idea generators that
you will adjust and adapt to the specific
needs of the children you are working
with in your classroom.

We hope you will enjoy using the
materials in this book as much as we
enjoyed preparing them.

T. D.
P. F.
R. G.
V. S.
J. S.

contents

Chapter 1
In the Beginning

The Philosopher

PHILOSOPHY

Concerned for the student as an individual? Like small-group interaction? Intrigued with children helping other children? Believe in different teaching styles for different learning styles? Want to cater to children's needs?

No labels? No categories? No high groups? No low groups? Can children become involved in learning, growing? Can children be trusted? Are they creative? Can they make choices? Can they be responsible for self-evaluation? Are they really human?

YES?
Five children doing ten different activities does not send you reeling? Busy noise does not bug you? Students moving about do not unnerve you?

Then learning centers can help you to personalize and individualize instruction. They can give children a choice. They can provide for different modes of learning. They can buy time, time for you to say to a child, face to face: "My, I like that. Tell me about it!"

Centers can have specific activities for specific skills. They can be self-checking. They can provide activities that are open-ended and that encourage divergent thinking.

The Role of the Teacher

What is the role of the teacher in the learning-center classroom? Decision maker? Planner? Organizer? Evaluator? Facilitator? Initiator? Friend?

The teacher's role is perhaps more important in the learning-center classroom than in any other classroom. The teacher's role must help him to know the child—how he learns, how he feels, how he thinks, how he operates. It must help him to discover the child's learning style, the concepts and skills the child needs to develop, the activities that can best meet his needs—that can help him grow. In the role of learning-center teacher, one must also determine how children's progress will be evaluated, how evaluation can be a joint venture between teacher and student, and how progress will be communicated to parents.

In short, the teacher's role is not one of passive bystander but of active participant. The teacher must be accountable.

A classroom can have all the trappings of openness and individualized instruction: nooks and crannies, attractive centers, clever furniture arrangement, books, supplies, kits, things, and kids on the move.

But, without change in the teacher's role, learning can be as structured and as manipulated as if students were in five rows, in three groups, with the teacher standing at the front of the room— teaching, keeping order, assigning chapters and workbook pages, asking literal questions, and announcing tests.

Your classroom is *your* classroom. *You* are the one who can choose to make it *with* kids! You need only to examine the alternatives, choices, and ideas that can help you. What should be your role? It must be choosing to:

facilitate
initiate
motivate
listen
encourage
develop
evaluate
record
introduce

What is a Center?

A learning center is an instructional device developed with a specific goal in mind. Activities are provided to reach an outcome (which could be different for each child).

A center can be:
designed for a purpose
designed for any number of activities
designed to introduce, develop, or
　　reinforce a concept
designed for a group or an individual
self-checking
designed for different ability and
　　achievement levels
goal- or skill-oriented
open-ended
just for fun
teacher-made or student-developed
set up for activities that are concrete or
　　abstract
assigned by a teacher
chosen by a student

STEPS IN DEVELOPING A CENTER

What must the teacher take into consideration when designing a center? Appearance and effect may be the key words in center design; however, the following ideas may be helpful:

1. Define skills, concepts to be learned or reinforced—or enjoyed. *What is haiku?*
2. Design learning activities or tasks that will reach goals. *These are examples of haiku. A haiku has these characteristics.*
3. Provide for extending activities.
　Write your own haiku.
　Put your haiku on a chart, or put it into the class booklet, to share with others.
　Research the origin of haiku.

Slowly!

Carefully!

INITIATING THE CENTER CLASSROOM

How do you achieve a center classroom? Very s–l–o–w–l–y and c–a–r–e–f–u–l–l–y! An excited, open teacher, the ultimate in materials and facilities, and a variety of learning centers may leave one important ingredient missing—the child! Can the child
work independently?
make worthwhile choices?
complete activities?
record progress?
work as a group member?

The skills of working as a team member, of making wise choices, of following directions, must be learned. These skills must be refined. They must be reinforced.

Children who have functioned in the so-called "traditional" classroom, who have always been told precisely what to do, who have always raised their hands to speak, and who have been lined up to walk down the halls can hardly make the transition to the flexible, self-disciplined learning-center classroom overnight.

In the early stages of the learning-center classroom it may be necessary to be somewhat structured to allow children to gradually develop self-direction, independence, and responsibility. Initially, one or two centers might be set up and used only at certain times. Then, discussion should be held with the class as to how and when the centers are to be used. Consider questions like: Is sequence of activities important? Is record keeping a part of the center? Are the centers *group* centers or *individual* centers? Do sign-up sheets need to be used? Will a "Center Open" or "Center Closed" sign be used?

Be sure to let the class identify standards that will be observed while using centers. Let the ideas come from them. Post the standards in chart form in a prominent place in the classroom. Refer to them when necessary: "John, you know that you helped to develop the standards."

AFTER CENTERS ARE INITIATED

Most teachers who are convinced that they "buy" the learning-center philosophy will, in the initial stages, develop one or two centers—a skill center, a center developed around a unit, or possibly a fun center containing games and manipulative activities.

This gives both the students and the teacher time to examine some important issues: What kind of record keeping will be used? How will centers be introduced—to the large group or to a small group? How about wise use of time and the ability of the student to make choices? Can students assist in making guidelines for classroom management?

When students are able to work independently, to work with others, to share, to plan their day, and to accept responsibilities, the teacher will be free to move toward more center use, or perhaps even to the total center concept.

Whether partial conversion or total conversion of centers is prevalent in the classroom, careful planning of center activities and evaluation of their effectiveness must be constant.

Considerations such as the following should be foremost:

Do the center activities relate to the specified objectives?

Are the center activities motivating?

Can the learners perform the activities independently?

Are the activities designed to introduce a new concept, reinforce a concept being taught, or review a concept previously taught?

Are there opportunities for self-discovery?

Are there opportunities for the learner to make a choice?

Does the learner understand what he is to do?

Is the learner experiencing success?

How do the children and the teacher operate in the classroom after the children have been oriented to the center concept?

First and foremost, children need to learn how to function independently. Teachers need to guide and plan with children in becoming self-directed and in being able to make decisions. Being able to work independently doesn't happen automatically without teacher assistance or within a given period. Much time needs to be spent helping children gain the skills and self-concept necessary for working independently.

The ways in which the teacher and the children operate are as varied as the personalities of the individuals. There is *no* step-by-step method of operating in centers. A few suggestions are listed here; the classroom teacher will have to modify these ideas to fit her own personality, her philosophy, and the capabilities of her students.

For example, suppose a departmentalized fifth grade is studying a unit on Japan. The children and the teacher have planned together the objectives that they hope to accomplish. At this point the teacher could present the students with a list of learning centers and descriptive activities from which they may select one or two. This way the teacher and the student can map out activities for the next six weeks or however long the unit on Japan will last. As each activity is completed, the student and teacher could have a conference to evaluate the student's progress and his ability to meet the specified objectives.

The centers need not be large or take up too much space. Center activities could be explained in folders filed in boxes or in a filing cabinet. Materials to be used for the activities could be kept in a closet or storage area. As children progress from center to center they could pull out needed materials and store them at the end of the period. Children could be involved in independent research, group projects, art work, and a variety of curriculum areas related to Japan.

An alternative to this situation would be for the teacher to set up as many centers on Japan as space in her room allowed. This could be done on a weekly basis or as long as the centers needed to be available to the students. Students could be given a list of activities available in each center and could sign up on a sheet at the center for the period and the activity or activities they wished to complete.

In a class where the teacher uses learning centers to supplement the regular program, manipulative games or activities in math, reading, science, and so on could be available on a table, in folders, on the bookshelf, or elsewhere for individuals who need reinforcement with certain skills. Answer sheets could be available for the appropriate activity for the individual to check his work immediately. Another student may be in charge of checking the work. The student may leave his work in a turn-in box or folder for the teacher to check or to keep up with his progress in certain skills.

A self-contained classroom affords many possibilities for center utilization. There may be centers available for each curriculum area, such as reading, math, and science. The teacher and children may discuss center activities at the beginning of each day, and children may move from center to center as they are ready and as centers are available. They may sign up for certain activities in advance. The teacher may keep a folder on each child in each subject area and check off the child's satisfactory completion of necessary skills to be developed. This allows the child to keep up with his own progress. Conferences between child and teacher should take place as often as necessary. These same arrangements have even greater possibilities in open-space, team-teaching situations in which large areas may be designated as curriculum centers (for science, math, and so on).

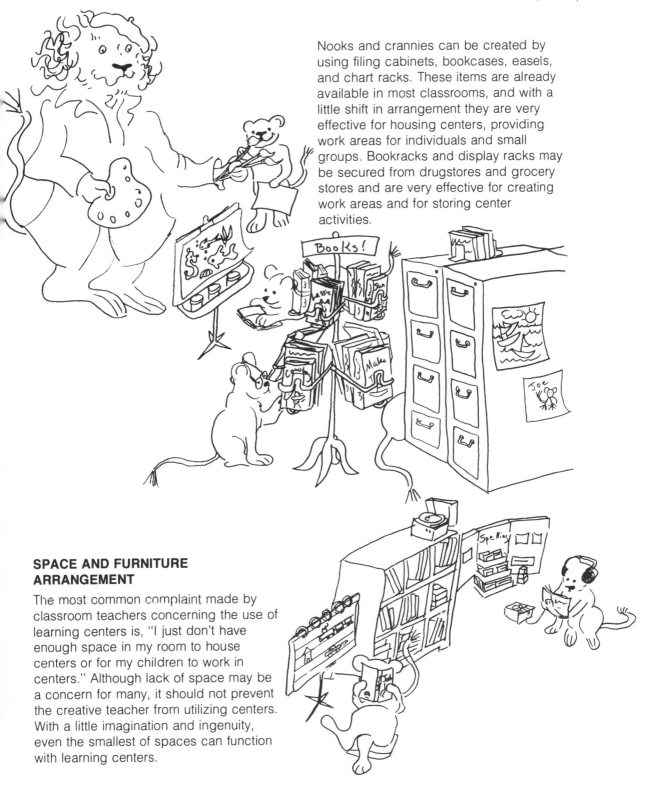

Nooks and crannies can be created by using filing cabinets, bookcases, easels, and chart racks. These items are already available in most classrooms, and with a little shift in arrangement they are very effective for housing centers, providing work areas for individuals and small groups. Bookracks and display racks may be secured from drugstores and grocery stores and are very effective for creating work areas and for storing center activities.

SPACE AND FURNITURE ARRANGEMENT

The most common complaint made by classroom teachers concerning the use of learning centers is, "I just don't have enough space in my room to house centers or for my children to work in centers." Although lack of space may be a concern for many, it should not prevent the creative teacher from utilizing centers. With a little imagination and ingenuity, even the smallest of spaces can function with learning centers.

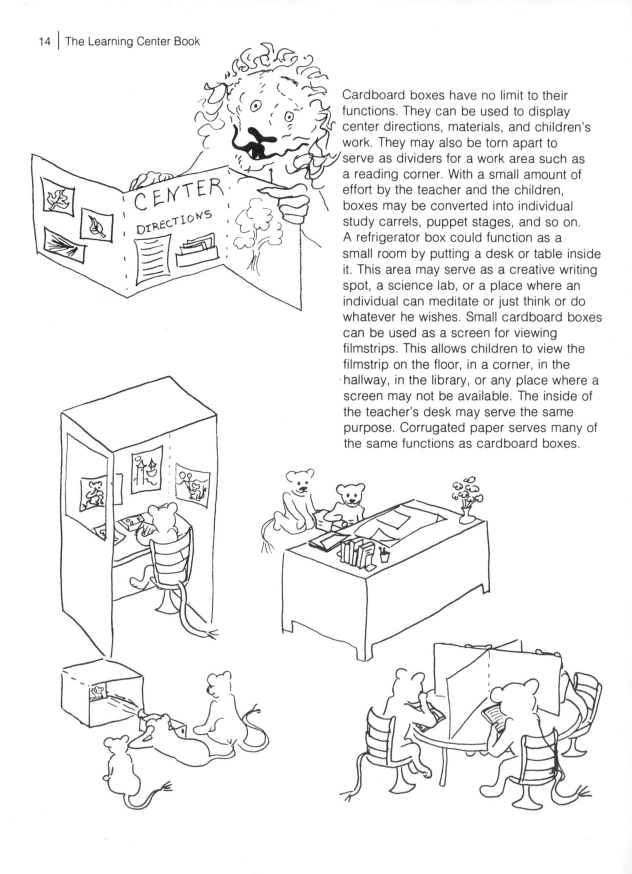

Cardboard boxes have no limit to their functions. They can be used to display center directions, materials, and children's work. They may also be torn apart to serve as dividers for a work area such as a reading corner. With a small amount of effort by the teacher and the children, boxes may be converted into individual study carrels, puppet stages, and so on. A refrigerator box could function as a small room by putting a desk or table inside it. This area may serve as a creative writing spot, a science lab, or a place where an individual can meditate or just think or do whatever he wishes. Small cardboard boxes can be used as a screen for viewing filmstrips. This allows children to view the filmstrip on the floor, in a corner, in the hallway, in the library, or any place where a screen may not be available. The inside of the teacher's desk may serve the same purpose. Corrugated paper serves many of the same functions as cardboard boxes.

Chalkboards, chalkboard ledges, and bulletin boards can house center activities and can be the answer to a space problem. Children's desks can be grouped around these areas when necessary, or individuals can sit and work on the floor utilizing these facilities.

The floor is very functional for the creative teacher. Children may sit on pillows, on throw rugs, or on the carpet. Many center tasks and activites can be taken to the floor by an individual or a small group. Some teachers have the idea that all activities must be completed within a center area. Tasks and activities should be planned so that children can work, as much as possible, in any space or area.

Children should be involved in designing work areas, dividers, centers, and so on when possible. Children should be allowed to utilize any available space, such as corners, floors, closets, halls, cafeteria, and library. The creative teacher can find a use for practically anything and never stops begging and borrowing items to use in her classroom. Space and furniture arrangement is not a problem for the imaginative and flexible teacher.

Backdrops made from paper or material can hang from the ceiling to provide work areas and to display children's work. The sinks, windows, window shades, doors, and closets have possibilities for center utilization. The ceiling is the limit for the creative teacher. The adventuresome teacher may even build a loft in the classroom to provide more work space.

Kinds of Centers

Skill Center — Prescriptive Center

As the name implies, the skill or prescriptive center's purpose is to develop or reinforce a specific skill. One of the best features of this center is that it can be adapted to the various levels of the students in the group. One student might be able to or need to complete three activities, while another would need to complete only two activities of a more advanced nature. This provides for individual differences within one center. Or, skill centers can be developed specifically for certain children. If, for example, five students need extensive work with vowels, a center can be developed for these students and their specific needs. Or, a skill center might be developed for a heterogeneous group. Then, a student who is working at a lower skill level could be tutored by another or could have the directions for his learning tasks read to him by a more skilled reader in the group.

Diagnostic or Inventory Center

The diagnostic or inventory center is designed for the specific purpose of answering these questions: What skills do the children have? What concepts have they mastered? Can they think critically? Can they make generalizations?

For example, a diagnostic or inventory center might examine whether the child has mastered his multiplication tables, vowel sounds, or map skills. This examination could determine the next route the child and teacher take in math, reading, or study skills.

Individual Study Center

In the individual study center, student and teacher select a topic that is of special interest to the student. Using a form of study guide, the student researches the topic, prepares notes, develops an outline, and finally makes a presentation to the class, orally or by a center. The student is evaluated on the extensiveness of his research, on his note-taking and outlining skills, and on his presentation to the large group (which could be in center form). The student, the teacher, and the class can participate in the evaluation.

The teacher should prepare a study guide or learning package for the child, keeping in mind such things as its readability level and the child's skill and concept development.

Draw a Map

Fun Centers

Not every activity in which the student engages has to have a clearly stated skill objective. Is school not a place to enjoy oneself? Why not have a hobby center, a dress-up center, a center with games, or one with a small puppet theater? Of course, there is the possibility that much can be learned in centers of this type, but what is to be learned is not specifically stated, nor are the outcomes precisely measured.

Student-Designed Center

A student-designed center could easily grow out of a student's independent study project or could occur as a takeoff from a group activity. The center could be used to share information or it could deal with issues a student found to be important in the independent study project or in his group project.

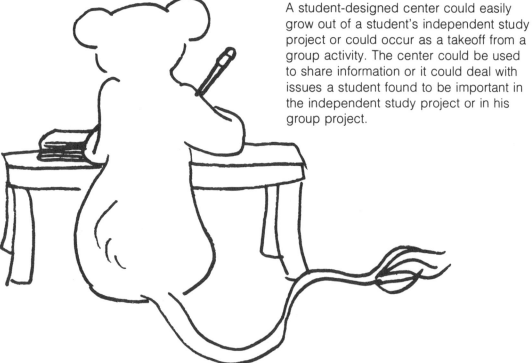

Commercial Center

Kits of multimedia nature, free materials, or programmed materials can be incorporated into centers. A kit on Mexico, for example, might deal with ideas, skills, concepts, and generalizations, and it could involve critical thinking. It is important to use kits and realia as an integral part of the program, not as a sideline or a supplement.

Evaluation

Teacher Key: What kind of growth has the student made in accordance with his interests and abilities?

Child Key: How do I feel about what I have achieved? What have I really learned? Did I reach my goals?

Evaluation is an ongoing process that is the responsibility of both child and teacher. A system should be tailor-made for the teacher and child to use continually. Evaluation begins when the child begins activities. The child should be able to evaluate work, determine progress, define weaknesses, and plan for future work. The teacher should maintain permanent records, note progress as well as weakness, identify areas for future work, and be able to report to parents. As a result, the child and his parents will have more information than could ever be given by an A, B, or C.

Record Keeping

Some teachers keep voluminous records. They operate best like this, or perhaps they have teacher or parent aides available to help. On the other hand, some teachers keep a minimum of records because this method suits their mode of operation.

What kinds of records can be kept?

1. *Center Checklist*—Kept by the teacher, she can see at a glance the centers that have been completed by each child.
2. *Student Folder*—Kept by the child, it gives information on centers completed.
3. *Master List*—Kept in a prominent place in the classroom, this list tells which students have chosen specific centers and what centers are still available for choice. A system of symbols could be developed for use with prereaders.
4. *Center Checksheet*—Kept at each center, a student signs his name and the date when he completes the work.
5. *Individual Folders*—Kept by the teacher, they could include skill checklists, centers completed, conference records, anecdotal records. This information can be used in parent-teacher conferences and for reporting periods.
6. *Anecdotal Records*—Kept by the teacher, the British refer to such material as the "living record"— information on the child's physical, mental, emotional, and social maturation. Anecdotal records are in addition to records in skill development but are of paramount importance when dealing with children as humans. They tell the teacher about the child as a person so she may deal with his human development.

The Conference

Perhaps the single most important aspect of learning-center teaching is the teacher-pupil conference. The teacher is saying to the child: "I am interested in you. I want to know what you are doing. Where are you successful? What are your problems? What can I do to help? Where do you think we should go next?"

Conferences can be set up on a regular basis according to a schedule. But there must be enough flexibility in the program to make time for a conference when the child or teacher feels it is necessary.

A good record-keeping system allows the teacher to have at his fingertips the information needed to assess development. A record of the individual conference is needed so that this information can be used in the next conference. With records from previous conferences, the teacher can say, "You seemed to be having trouble with completing your work in addition of fractions the last time we talked. Do you feel better about it now? Let's see what improvement you have made."

STUFF FOR A WORKING ENVIRONMENT

Furniture usage
Movable furniture can make nooks and
crannies to be used as:
places to hide
places to work in groups
quiet, cozy spaces
noisy spaces
storage spaces
places to rest
places to discover

Things: Furniture
lofts (yes, built right in the room)
cardboard boxes
refrigerator crates
window shades
venetian blinds
rolling carts
tables
movable desks
bulletin boards
art easels
rugs
rocking chairs
benches
chairs
bookcases
bookracks
cots
hammocks
chart stands
sides of cabinets
closets
portable boards

Things: Materials
texts
trade books
art supplies
musical instruments
looms
community specialists (people)
modes
realia
picture material
games
maps, globes
cooking equipment
AV equipment:
    record player
    listening posts

cassettes
overhead projector
opaque projector
transparencies
microfilm
camera
films
film loops
phonograph records
copy machines
laminating equipment
VTR
slides
filmstrips

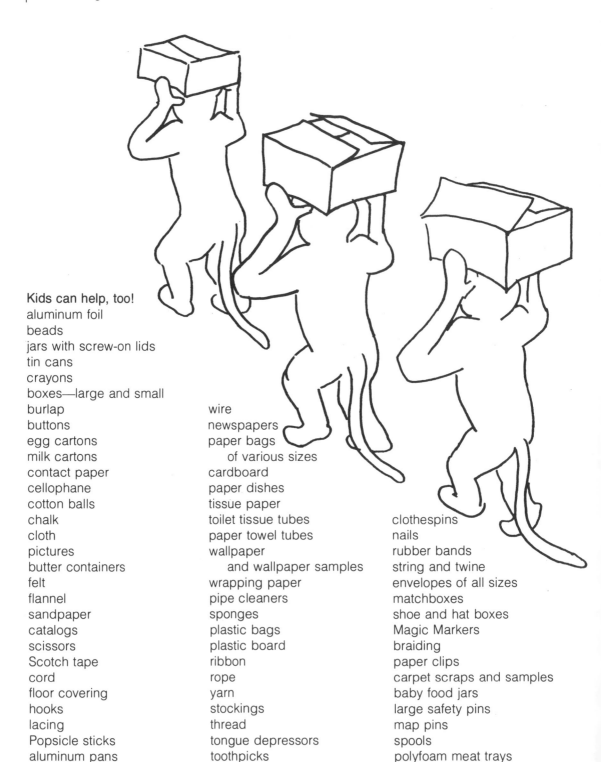

Kids can help, too!

aluminum foil
beads
jars with screw-on lids
tin cans
crayons
boxes—large and small
burlap
buttons
egg cartons
milk cartons
contact paper
cellophane
cotton balls
chalk
cloth
pictures
butter containers
felt
flannel
sandpaper
catalogs
scissors
Scotch tape
cord
floor covering
hooks
lacing
Popsicle sticks
aluminum pans

wire
newspapers
paper bags
    of various sizes
cardboard
paper dishes
tissue paper
toilet tissue tubes
paper towel tubes
wallpaper
    and wallpaper samples
wrapping paper
pipe cleaners
sponges
plastic bags
plastic board
ribbon
rope
yarn
stockings
thread
tongue depressors
toothpicks

clothespins
nails
rubber bands
string and twine
envelopes of all sizes
matchboxes
shoe and hat boxes
Magic Markers
braiding
paper clips
carpet scraps and samples
baby food jars
large safety pins
map pins
spools
polyfoam meat trays

plastic vegetable baskets
brads
toothbrushes
gallon ice cream cartons (round)
soft-drink cans
rickrack
corrugated cardboard
things from nature
    seeds, leaves, acorns, pine cones,
        rocks, weeds, egg shells
sawdust
styrofoam
straws
paper doilies
wax paper
lace
drinking cups (paper, styrofoam)
steel wool
food coloring
construction paper
macaroni
stapler
Q-tips
cigar boxes
coffee tins
Band-aid tins
buttons
cork
screen
coat hangers
mesh vegetable and fruit sacks
magazines
orange juice containers
plastic measuring spoons
plastic measuring cups
funnels
screws
bolts
balloons
balls (ping pong, tennis, golf)
screen wire (small pieces)
plastic turkey basters
can lids
material scraps
shoe bags

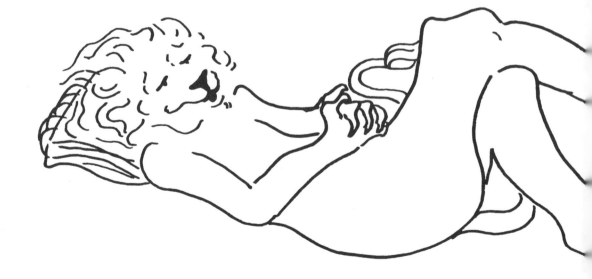

Now remember,
    integrate subject matter!

Speaking

Listening

Reading

Writing

Chapter 2
In Language Arts

Planning to develop learning centers in the language arts
should include the following activities: Speaking
Listening
Reading
Writing
Spelling

However, many or all of the center ideas presented in this chapter
could easily be adapted to or integrated into any of the other discipline
areas. The various centers can be used at any grade level, but examples
have been shown at the early childhood and elementary grade levels.
And all have been tested in classroom environments.

The Funny Farm

WHAT'S IT FOR?

To review and reinforce new vocabulary words on plant unit in science.

STUFF YOU'LL NEED
- construction paper
- poster board
- markers
- tape
- display board or box
- mimeographed sheets
- seeds
- mimeographed calendars
- plain paper
- plant flash cards

HOW'S IT WORK?

Children may select any activity to begin with; no sequence is necessary.

1. *Leaf Fun*—Children take a mimeographed sheet of scrambled letters and arrange them correctly to spell plant words.
2. *Fun Forest*—Children pretend to be a redwood tree that is 269 years old. They write a short story describing events of their lifetime.
3. *The Art Garden*—Students make a seed collage.
4. *Tool Shed*—Using plant flash cards and calendars, students figure out when vegetables will be ready.
5. & 6. *Fun Activities*—Students find and circle plant words in a jumble of letters.

HOW'D THEY DO?

Activities 1, 2, and 4 have hand-in instructions.
Activity 3 is displayed.
Activities 5 and 6 may be observed for evaluation.

FIT'N IT IN

Science—Vocabulary in "Leaf Fun" and "Tool Shed" could come from science texts.
Art—The "Art Garden" collage could be made after techniques and steps in making a collage are demonstrated.

Nyms—Synonyms, Antonyms, and Homonyms

WHAT'S IT FOR?

To develop understanding of the structure of
   words and their meanings.
To encourage creativity.
To provide "fun" activities when spare time is
   available.

STUFF YOU'LL NEED

- construction paper
- poster paper
- plywood and hinges (display board)
- cans
- Magic Markers
- tape
- stapler
- scissors
- folders
- dictionary
- books
- newspapers
- various games

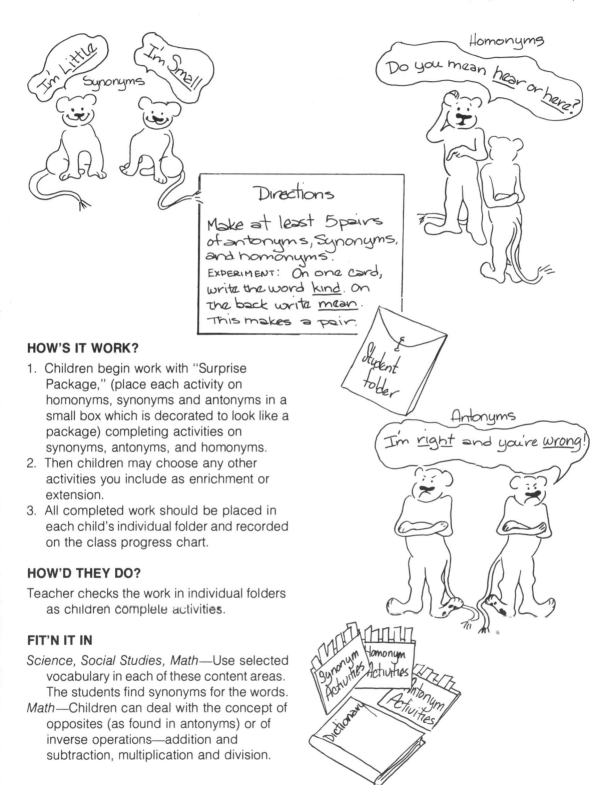

Synonyms

I'm Little

I'm Small

Homonyms

Do you mean _hear_ or _here_?

Directions

Make at least 5 pairs of antonyms, synonyms, and homonyms.

EXPERIMENT: On one card, write the word _kind_. On the back write _mean_. This makes a pair.

Student folder

Antonyms

I'm _right_ and you're _wrong_!

HOW'S IT WORK?

1. Children begin work with "Surprise Package," (place each activity on homonyms, synonyms and antonyms in a small box which is decorated to look like a package) completing activities on synonyms, antonyms, and homonyms.
2. Then children may choose any other activities you include as enrichment or extension.
3. All completed work should be placed in each child's individual folder and recorded on the class progress chart.

HOW'D THEY DO?

Teacher checks the work in individual folders as children complete activities.

FIT'N IT IN

Science, Social Studies, Math—Use selected vocabulary in each of these content areas. The students find synonyms for the words.

Math—Children can deal with the concept of opposites (as found in antonyms) or of inverse operations—addition and subtraction, multiplication and division.

Synonym Activities

Homonym Activities

Antonym Activities

Dictionary

Look What's Cooking

WHAT'S IT FOR?

To develop understanding of prefixes and their meanings.
To develop skill in recognizing prefixes and root words.
To develop skill in using prefixes and root words.

STUFF YOU'LL NEED

- display board
- envelopes
- Magic Markers
- scissors
- glue
- tape
- stapler
- boxes
- poster paper

HOW'S IT WORK?

Children begin with activity number 1 and complete each activity in sequence through number 8.

1. Examine definition of the term prefix; look at some common prefixes and their meanings.
2. Identify the prefix for each of several words and place them in an envelope.
3. Make words with the prefix wheel.
4. Examine other prefixes and definitions.
5. Examine definitions of root words and change root words listed by adding a prefix.
6. Play root word "fish" game.
7. Read a story that is provided. Underline the prefixes once and circle root words.
8. Correct work in number 7 with answer key and put papers in envelopes.

HOW'D THEY DO?

Let children working in the center compare and evaluate each other's work. Work to be checked by the teacher is placed in envelopes.

FIT'N IT IN

Math—Utilize math vocabulary from unit being studied (multiplication, division, etc.).

Science—With the addition of prefixes to root words, a student can make many new science words.

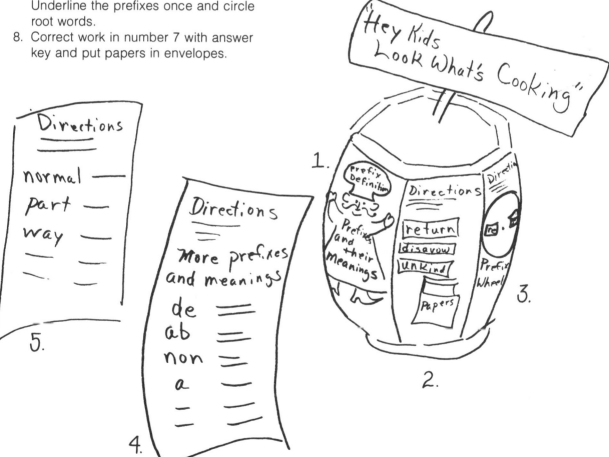

All Aboard!
Reading Center

WHAT'S IT FOR?

To develop concepts of sentences.
To develop skill in sequencing.
To give practice in reading.

STUFF YOU'LL NEED

- poster board
- box
- envelopes
- word cards with a hole punched in the center top
- six-car train made of construction paper
- hooks
- paper for passenger list
- engineer's hat

HOW'S IT WORK?

This center is set up in a train motif. Children follow directions posted in the center to make sentences on the train. After completion, the children add their names to a passenger list provided in the center.

HOW'D THEY DO?

Use passenger list to check on which children visited the center.
Were the directions clear?
Did children on all levels find the activity stimulating?
What check on children's sentences was there? Is one needed?

L&N Railroad Co.
list of passengers

In this center you can...
1. get a ticket
2. put on the hat
3. open ticket envelope - make a sentence from the cards you find there
4. add your name to the list of travelers

hook or nail

FIT'N IT IN

Reading—The ticket envelope could contain a sequence story to be put in order.

Math—Fractions on separate cards could be put in order from smallest to largest. Pictures of objects with different sizes, lengths, and widths could be placed in order.

Spelling—Spelling words could be used to make sentences.

Dictionary—Alphabetizing could be done by placing five or six cards in envelopes to be alphabetized on the train hooks.

The Girelephiger*
Spelling Center

WHAT'S IT FOR?

To develop skills in critical thinking and problem solving.

To develop skill in visualizing the spelling of words.

STUFF YOU'LL NEED

- poster paper
- pail or other container
- markers
- slips of paper
- direction sheet
- answer sheet

HOW'S IT WORK?

Make a poster-paper animal with the head of an elephant, the body of a tiger, and the legs of a giraffe. Attach a container to the trunk of the animal to hold slips of paper containing scrambled spelling words plus a clue (*example: WASYLA*—Use these letters to make a word meaning "all the time"). Children take a slip of paper from the pail and follow the directions posted in the center. They unscramble the spelling words, then check their list against a master list posted somewhere in the room.

(*part giraffe, elephant, and tiger)

HOW'D THEY DO?

To learn who has completed the activity, provide an envelope at the same place as the list of correct answers.

Did the children feel free to get help from adults or other students when they got stuck on a word?

Did particular words cause extra difficulty?

FIT'N IT IN

Math—Put scrambled equations in the pail.
Social Studies—Scramble vocabulary words in the current unit. Scramble names of community helpers and their jobs.
Music—Scramble words from songs.

SOMEBODY GOOFED, THERE'S NO DOUBT ABOUT IT.
I'M SO SCRAMBLED UP I WANTED TO SHOUT IT.
THEY GAVE ME THIS PAIL WITH MIXED-UP WORDS IN IT.
THEY SAID YOU COULD FIX THEM IN LESS THAN A MINUTE.

1. Number your paper from 1 to 12.
2. Take a slip of paper from the Girelephiger and unscramble the word on your paper beside the correct number.
3. Check your completed list with the one posted on the filing cabinet.

Scrambled Spelling Words

Bookmaker's Center

Once upon a time...

WHAT'S IT FOR?

To develop skills in putting stories in sequence.

To develop the recognition that books are stories someone made up, wrote down, and had pictures drawn for.

To promote originality.

STUFF YOU'LL NEED

- poster paper
- construction paper
- newsprint
- crayons
- markers
- stapler
- three styrofoam balls
- flat styrofoam base
- coal
- scarf and small broomstick

HOW'S IT WORK?

Make a snowman from styrofoam, using coal for features. Children come to the center, choose a story title from under the snowman's hat, and dictate it to an adult or older child. (Possible titles: "The Snowman Who Has a Heart," "The Boy Who Talked to the Cold North Wind," "The Day Ice Covered the City," "Here Come the Snowplows," "The Biggest Snowman Ever," "The Girl Who Had Never Seen Snow.") The story is then put in book form, as illustrated.

Illustrations are drawn on each page according to what part of the story is on that page. The words on each page will have to be read to prereaders. Staple the finished book. During group time children read their books to the class (the teacher can do it in the case of prereaders).

HOW'D THEY DO?

Children make a bookworm head and add a section to its body each time they complete a book. By glancing at bookworms mounted around the room the teacher can see who has been participating in bookmaking.

Compare children's latest efforts with earlier ones.

Which subjects under the hat got the best responses?

Was sufficient time set aside for sharing stories?

Was there enough adult or older child help?

FIT'N IT IN

Math—Have students write another winter story using as many number words as they can. Sample titles: "Too Many Overshoes," "How Many Snowmen?"

Social Studies—Use titles that reflect the current unit of study: "The Snow Workers," "No Snowplows," "The Postman in the Snow."

Science—Use science-oriented titles: "How Cold Is Cold?" "An Icicle Is Melting," "How It Feels To Be a Snowflake."

Music—Children listen to music that sounds like cold wind, snow falling, and so on, and they write about how they feel as they listen.

Health—Provide story titles like "I Have a Cold," "What Happens When You Cough?" "How to Catch a Cold."

Safety—Use story titles such as "Walking on Ice," "The Snowball Fight," "Lost in a Snowstorm."

Seasonal and Holidays—Story titles could center around winter holidays—Christmas, New Year's, first day of winter.

The No Lyin' Lion
Speaking Center

WHAT'S IT FOR?

To provide opportunities for children to express themselves in a story.
To develop children's skills in "reading" a picture, then filling in their own details in story form.

STUFF YOU'LL NEED

- tape recorder
- large poster-paper lion
- six to eight colorful, interesting pictures

HOW'S IT WORK?

A tape recorder the children can operate is placed on a table in the center. Over it is hung the lion, with a pocket full of pictures.

Children choose a picture that sparks their imagination, and they tape a story about the picture.

Stories are played back for small groups or the whole class.

HOW'D THEY DO?

Use group time to discuss taping stories to get feedback from children.

Was the tape recorder easy to use for all children?

What skills need to be built as a result of this center (diagnostic)?

Did children feel a sense of accomplishment and self-worth from this task?

FIT'N IT IN

Social Studies—Use pictures of community helpers at work, famous landmarks in America or in other countries, famous Americans, and legendary characters.

Music—Children sing a song that goes with the pictures they choose.

Reading—The lion's pocket could have a picture from a current reading story.

Spelling—The lion's pocket could contain spelling words to create stories with.

Math—Provide numerically oriented pictures for counting stories.

I'm Not Lyin'

Choose a picture!
Tape a story!

My Pocket is full of fun!

Sounds
We Know
Listening Center

WHAT'S IT FOR?

To develop listening skills required to identify sounds in visual form.
To develop the recognition that eyes and ears work together.

STUFF YOU'LL NEED

- ten to twelve laminated pictures depicting various sounds recorded on tape
- tape recorder—cassette if possible

HOW'S IT WORK?

Make tapes of a variety of sounds. Include the sound of a fire engine, jet plane, car horn, water running, dishwasher running, Coke poured over ice, dog barking, door shutting, scissors cutting paper, telephone ringing.
Scatter the pictures around the center. Children listen to the tape and take turns holding up the picture that illustrates the sound they hear.

HOW'D THEY DO?

Was this activity too difficult or too easy? Did it draw children of all abilities? Was there room to manipulate pictures?

FIT'N IT IN

Math—Record sounds of a certain number of claps that children use with a worksheet or number board.
Music—Rhythms on a tom-tom are recorded; children reproduce exactly what they hear.
Science—Animal sounds must be matched up with animal pictures.
Social Studies—Record sounds to match up with community helpers or sounds of tools being used to match up with pictures of tools.

Create A Mystery

HOW'S IT WORK?

Children may choose from the following activities:

1. *Tape a Mystery*—A child or a group of children dictate a mystery onto the tape recorder. They may include sound effects.
2. *Mystery Bones*—Children examine animal bones and write a mystery around them.
3. *End a Mystery*—Children listen to the taped first half of a mystery and create their own ending.
4. *Detective Snoop's File*—The student reads a mystery book and completes a record card, which he puts in a file box. He puts his fingerprint on the card.

HOW'D THEY DO?

Efforts may be evaluated by taped mystery stories, completed work handed in to the teacher (who might use a hand-in box), and completed book cards.

WHAT'S IT FOR?

To encourage children to express themselves orally and in writing.

STUFF YOU'LL NEED

- tape recorder
- blank tapes
- prerecorded mystery story
- ink pad
- animal bones (real or pictures)
- file box
- 3" x 5" cards

FIT'N IT IN

Music—Challenge children to create and record mysterious sounding backgrounds for their mystery stories.

Spelling—Create a mysterious spelling list made up of mystery-type words, such as conceal, mystify, secret, suspense, and so on.

A Nose for News

WHAT'S IT FOR?

To develop understanding of the make-up of a newspaper.

To develop recognition of the types of newspaper articles found in daily newspapers.

STUFF YOU'LL NEED

- display board
- poster paper
- boxes
- Magic Markers
- glue
- tape
- stapler
- games
- art materials
- different types of newspaper articles

HOW'S IT WORK?

Children should complete learning activities in sequence.

1. Children play a spelling scrabble game using newspaper terminology and/or do a crossword puzzle using terms.
2. Child draws a cartoon (political or social) or a comic strip for a newspaper.
3. Children read different types of articles and classify them as to types. Then, they answer questions concerning types of articles.
4. Working in pairs, one child is a reporter and one child draws a card telling him who he is. The reporter interviews the person and together they write an article on the interview.

HOW'D THEY DO?

All written material should be evaluated by the teacher.
Art work may be displayed.
Children may share, compare, and evaluate each other's work.

FIT'N IT IN

Social Studies—Children can study newspapers and develop an understanding of current events.
Creative Arts—Children could draw political cartoons and illustrations for their articles.

Imagination Magic

WHAT'S IT FOR?

To motivate the children to read more.
To get the children to use their imagination and do creative writing.
To make language arts enjoyable for the students.

STUFF YOU'LL NEED

- boxes
- folders
- tagboard
- crayons
- newsprint
- grease pencil
- word cards
- tape recorder and tape

MAIL BOX

7.

Sell
under ground hog
taker
6.

over
round

is made
made

un d
sp like able
s

4.

5.

Bill and Sue went exploring

HOW'S IT WORK?

Children may choose any activity to begin or may be directed to specific activities.

1. *Matching Game*—The children match the picture with the name of the picture.
2. *Word Builder*—The children take parts of words and form other words.
3. *Imaginary Trip in the Flying Trunk*—The children write and illustrate a creative story about their adventure in the trunk.
4. *Pick Flowers from the Flower Garden*—The children are given a root word and they add letters to the petals to form a complete flower.
5. *Hearts*—A word card game in which the children must be able to know how a word can be used in a sentence and its meaning in order to play.
6. *Tic-tac-toe*—A word game in which the children use their knowledge of combining words to make compound words.
7. *The Mailbox*—Used to inform students which activities they need to do and also to get the students' opinion of the activities they have completed.

HOW'D THEY DO?

Base evaluation on observation of the students as they use the center, worksheets that are turned in, comments of the students that are received in the mailbox, improved attitudes of the students toward reading and other things related to language arts, and stories the students write and illustrate.

FIT'N IT IN

Have children apply skills developed in this center in other curriculum areas.

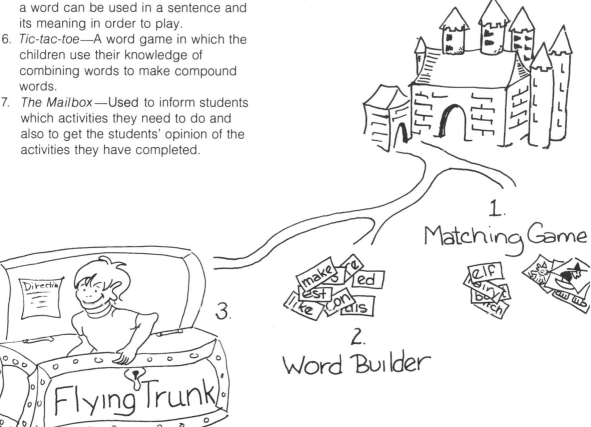

What does it really mean?

WHAT'S IT FOR?

To develop and reinforce critical thinking and reading skills.

STUFF YOU'LL NEED

- display board
- construction paper
- poster paper
- markers
- tape
- stapler
- tape recorders
- blank tapes
- prerecorded tapes
- study prints
- filmstrips
- film
- newspaper articles

HOW'D THEY DO?

All written work may be evaluated by the teacher.
Children may share work with each other.

FIT'N IT IN

Have students apply new critical thinking skills learned in this center to other curriculum areas, especially social science.

HOW'S IT WORK?

Children may begin with an activity of their choice and then complete others in any sequence.

1. Children view a study print and then read articles for and against breaking horses. They then make a list of for's and against's.
2. Children view the filmstrip, *The American Revolution,* and write one paragraph as a Britisher.
3. Children view the film, *How the West Was Won,* and prepare an advertisement encouraging attendance at the film.
4. Children listen to a tape-recorded speech, then list as many facts from the speech as possible.
5. Children listen to two tape-recorded messages, each of which uses voice inflection and tone to give a different message on the same topic. Children then read a paragraph on tape using their voices to affect meaning.
6. Children read several newspaper articles and list facts and opinions from them.

more ideas
in Language Arts Centers

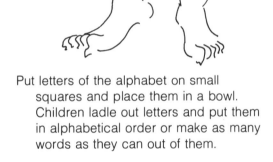

READING CENTERS

Make rebus stories for children to decipher.

Write stories in code using dots for alphabet letters. Give children a copy of the code; they decipher the story.

Write the days of the week on flash cards and the abbreviations for the days of the week on other flashcards. Children match the abbrevations to the written word.

Make a chart to help children with initial consonants. Laminate or contact the chart so it can be wiped off.
Example:
1. A duck has big (beet, feet).
2. A (dish, fish) likes to swim.
3. A (tire, fire) is hot.

Children cross out the word in parentheses that does not belong, then they check their work with an answer sheet.

Write words that rhyme separately on 3 x 5 cards and shuffle them. Children ask each other for the word that rhymes with their word.

Put letters of the alphabet on small squares and place them in a bowl. Children ladle out letters and put them in alphabetical order or make as many words as they can out of them.

Cut comic strips out of newspapers and make them into books for fun reading.

Make flash cards (two sets), one with contractions and the other with the two words that make up the contraction. Children match the two.

Make Mr. Peek-a-Boo, a clown cut out of poster paper and attached by the top of his hat to another piece of construction paper with a brad. On the hidden paper put sentences or words. When Mr. Peek-a-Boo is moved to the side for a few brief seconds, the children get a quick look and then tell what they read there.

Laminate or contact a set of pictures and prepare a word or phrase for each picture. Put these two sets into a center for children to match up the words with the pictures.

Cut cardboard circles (or any shape) in half with a jigsaw pattern. Write a word on one half and its antonym on the other half. Children match the puzzle pieces.

Prepare bingo cards, filling squares with words such as "happy," "over," "high," "before." The caller draws cards that have the antonyms on them. When he calls a word, a player can cover the antonym if it is on his card. The first player to complete a row is the winner and next caller.

Cut out poster-paper or construction-paper fish and put on them letters of the alphabet, words in a spelling or reading lesson, numbers, or anything else you wish to teach. Make a fish pond on the floor or in a shallow box (perhaps painted blue). Make a fishing pole out of a dowel to which yarn and a magnet are attached. Children throw the fishing line into the pond and tell what fish they catch. Put a paper clip on the fish's nose so the magnet will pick it up.

Prepare a set of ABC's that have holes in the top or a yarn loop for hanging. Put nails in the back of a bookcase or in a board, or stick pins in a bulletin board or on a piece of ceiling tile so that the children can line up the cards in order. Provide a chart of the correct sequence of the alphabet so those who aren't sure of the order can refer to it; others can check their work by it.

Prepare sandpaper letters or letters made of yarn glued on poster paper for children to trace with their fingers while saying the name of the letter.

Make an alphabet train—an engine and twenty-six cards on which are written the letters of the alphabet. Let the children put the alphabet in order.

Put ABC blocks in a center for children to use in spelling their names or in making words.

Make letters of the alphabet out of construction paper cut to about 4" x 6". Run yarn in a hole at the center top of each letter and tie around the children's necks. Call the children by this letter-name all day. The first day this is done it might be fun to let each child's name letters be his initials, so John Smith would have J.S. on his necklace and be called J.S. all day.

Pour a box of Alpha-bits cereal into several small bowls. Children try to spell words they know or their names with the cereal. Glue the word to colored construction paper.

Mount newspaper articles on construction paper and put them in a center with directions to circle all the S's or all the T's. This activity can be done in other ways—for example, circle all the the's or all the prepositions.

Make and laminate or contact a set of bingo cards with letters in the squares. On twenty-six small squares of construction paper put the letters of the alphabet for the caller to draw one at a time. Provide something for the players to cover their boards with.

Make an alphabet book. Children draw one letter on each page, then cut something from a magazine that starts with that letter. A minibook could be made by cutting newsprint small and stapling together the pages. On the A page children cut and paste all the letter A's, on the B page they cut and paste all the letter B's they can find in magazines, and so on.

Play Peek-a-Boo:

1. Choose a large colorful picture that lends itself easily to description—color, motion, size, shapes, and so on.
2. Paste it on a piece of construction paper. Over the picture place a second piece of construction paper the same size and attach the two pieces at the top with tape.
3. Cut small "windows" or flaps at strategic points in the top piece of paper. (places that will give clues as to what picture lies beneath). Number the windows in the order in which you want children to peek into the windows.
4. Ask children to gather around you for discussion.
5. Ask one child at a time to peek into window number 1 and tell the group what he sees. Help him "describe" it. Continue until all the windows have been opened and described.
6. The words or sentences that the children use may be recorded on a large chart or chalkboard by the teacher.

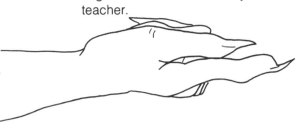

7. When all of the windows have been opened, the children try to guess what the picture is.
8. Show the picture to the children and let them see if they guessed right.
9. The teacher may write a short story about the picture using the words and sentences the children used to describe it. Then the story is read to the children.

Print name cards for various objects in the room and pictures on the wall. Flash a card and choose one child to touch the object or picture indicated. Call attention to the first letter sound in each word.

The card game "going fishing" can be modified to reinforce sight vocabulary. The deck of cards is a set of word cards, with each card containing one of the words the children are currently learning or have learned. There are two of each word in a set of cards and the object is to collect pairs. The players take turns asking each other for specific word cards.

Use the newspaper as a comprehension booster. Provide several questions that can be answered only by reading newspaper ads. The children read the ads and locate the necessary information.

Make a duck and several eggs from construction paper. On some of the eggs list words (or paste pictures) that are somehow related to the farm; the rest should feature objects that have nothing to do with farms. Challenge the children to separate the "farm eggs" from the others. Other possible themes for the same kind of classifying activity are the firehouse, the supermarket, and the garage.

Use "Scramble" to get your students to use and enhance their word power. Just get yourself a slew of two-inch blocks of wood and print a different letter of the alphabet on each side of each cube. Put the blocks in a container. To play the game, a child dumps the blocks out and tries to create words with the letters that show.

Make a game of compound learning. Print compound words on small index cards and then cut the two parts of each word apart. Mix up the cards and challenge the children to create compound words out of the mix. Each time a child finds a match, he writes down the resulting word. Later, he checks his work in a dictionary.

Supply your reading centers with plenty of crossword puzzles, as they provide great incentive for learning word meanings. Introduce crosswords with the simple left-to-right variety—the kind that go up-and-down as well can come later. And why not encourage your students to create their own crossword puzzles, too?

SPEAKING CENTERS

Have students use a shoe box, carpet scraps, and construction paper to construct scenes that depict a familiar story, a story they have made up, or the current reading story. They tell the story using the shadow box to illustrate it.

Have children illustrate a story they have made up, a familiar fairy tale, or the current reading story vertically on a long piece of newsprint (newspapers give away the ends of paper rolls).

Make a television out of a box with cut-to-size broom handles for rollers. After drawing the frames and putting in the illustrations, children attach the story to the rollers. They tell the story they illustrated as they turn it on the T.V. screen.

Put together a group of interesting pictures. Children choose a picture from the center and describe it to the other children there. This could also be done as a guessing game. The children could look over all the pictures in the center; then the describer would gather them up and put them out of sight. He would then pick one to describe and the others would guess which picture was being described.

Make a dramatization center. A group of children plan and act out a story they are familiar with. How elaborate they make it depends on their own creativity and on what props the center is equipped with. A center full of hats is a great come-on for young actors and actresses.

Play "You Have a Face." This game can be played in a large group or in a center. Make the center colorful by having large pictures of faces placed all over or on a piece of poster paper. The game starts with one child saying to another, "You have a face." The other answers, "What kind of face?" Then, starting with A and continuing through the alphabet, the child describes the face. For example, "You have an attractive face, you have a beautiful face, you have a cute face," and so on.

Put words (such as cap, hat, fan, dog, cat, pig, jet, car, cow, bug, fox, pin) on cards, one word to a card. Children draw a card and describe the word until the other children guess what it is. This game can be used with spelling words that are nouns. When the children guess what the word is, they then have to spell it correctly.

Tape up tongue twisters for children to repeat. Examples:
As the roaring rocket rose, the restless roosters rollicked.
A noisy noise annoys an oyster.
Cows graze in green grass which grows great.
The big black bumblebee.
Slippery seals slipping silently ashore.
A skunk jumped over a stump in a skunk hole.
She sells sea shells by the seashore.
Sister Susie's sewing shirts for soldiers.

Make a tall pipe or telescope from a cardboard cylinder roll and cover it with contact paper or wallpaper. Children can use it as a new way to talk to each other. Used as a telescope, children can look through it and describe what they see other children doing.

Buy two copies of familiar fairy tale books and cut them up. Mount the important scenes (the second book will let you use a good picture that was on the back of another one you needed) on poster paper and laminate them or cover them with clear contact. Children line up the cards according to the way they want the story to go, then they tell the story looking at the cards for clues. Also, old textbooks can be used for story scenes, and the children can make up stories to go with them.

Tape children speaking in whole sentences—who they are, where they live, what their phone number is, what they want for Christmas, what they want to be when they grow up, what their favorite food is, and so on.

Prepare task cards about opposites. The following activities could be read by one child and answered by another.

1. I will say a sentence. You say the same sentence using an opposite in it.
I saw a big dog. *(I saw a little dog.)*
I have a black piece of paper.
    (I have a white piece of paper.)
I went over a high hill.
I see something very soft.
The balloon went up.
The dog came in.
The train went very slow.
Put this on the top shelf.
The man is very short.
The soup is very cold.
I see an old man.
Here is a little cup.
The window is very low.
He put the hat on the top shelf.
My hands are hot.

2. Finish my sentence.
Snow is cold, fire is_____.
Sand is dry, water is _____.
People walk, birds _____.
The sun shines in the day, the moon shines at _____.
A dog is an animal, an apple is a _____.
A snail is slow, a rabbit is _____.
Dogs have hair, birds have _____.
A tree is a plant, a giraffe is an _____.

More opposites to make sentences with are hello/goodbye, asleep/awake, begin/end, go/stay, noisy/quiet, glad/sad, left/right, day/night, empty/full, loud/quiet, cold/hot, bright/dim, thin/fat, open/shut.

Give children sentences to finish.

As fast as _____.
As happy as _____.
As hot as _____.
As quiet as _____.
As tall as _____.
As sad as _____.
As cold as _____.
As loud as _____.
When I am alone I feel_____.
Every day my mother _____.
At school the kids like _____.
When it's my birthday I always _____.
My sister is always _____.
When it rains it makes me want to _____.

Make a telephone out of cans and heavy string. Put holes in the center of the bottom of the cans to tie the strings securely to. The children must hold the string taut for voices to be transmitted from one can to the other.

Display pictures showing different kinds of pollution as well as some clean environment pictures. Children answer questions such as: What is the difference in these pictures? What do you think caused this difference? Which pictures show places you would like to live in? What can we do about pollution? Children prepare to answer in an oral report to the class.

LISTENING CENTERS

Record the following:
I am going to say four words. One of them does not belong in the group.

See if you can tell me the one that does not belong before I say it.
Red, green, blue, hat.
   (Pause) That's right, hat.
Cat, dog, mitten, rabbit.
   (Pause) Yes, it's mitten.
Boat, car, man, wagon.
   (Pause) Man is the answer.
Orange, pear, bell, apple.
   (Pause) A bell's not a fruit.
Beet, potatoes, chair, tomato.
   (Pause) That's right, chair.
Table, chair, sun, desk.
   (Pause) Yes, it's sun.
Sun, moon, star, flower.
   (Pause) Flower is the answer.
Rose, peach, pear, apple.
   (Pause) Yes, rose is not a fruit.
Pink, red, yellow, shoe.
   (Pause) Shoe doesn't belong here.
Dress, shirt, car, skirt.
   (Pause) That's right, car.

This listening game can be used in a center with a worksheet or with simple directions to write down the word that doesn't belong in the group. Students can also call the answer out loud to each other perhaps, alternating turns.

Play a simple game that incorporates two listening games in one. You need only two to four children and a prepared tape that gives directions such as these: "Each of you has a number, 1 or 2 or 3 or 4. When I call out your number, say out loud what sound you are hearing: number 2 (hands clapping sound), number 1 (snapping fingers), number 4 (knocking on door), number 3 (humming), number 1 (tapping feet), number 4 (coughing), number 2 (whistling), number 3 (crying)." This set of sounds is easy, so add progressively harder sounds as the tape continues.

Use the following poem for a simple game children can play in the listening center:

Little Tommy Tittlemouse living in a little house
Someone's knocking, me oh, my, someone's calling:
WHO AM I?

All the children in the center say the first two lines to a child who is facing away from the group, perhaps seated in a chair or on the floor. The "Who Am I" part is said by an unidentified child who comes up behind the seated child and says the line close up behind his head. The seated child tries to identify him by the sound of his voice only.

Use felt cutouts on a flannelboard to accompany a tape that gives such directions as: "Put the tree under the rabbit," "Put the circle beside the tree," "Put the sun over the house," and so on. Seasonal and holiday scenes can be used effectively in this center.

Prepare a tape as follows:

Do exactly as I say. Clap your hands two times. Ready, go. [pause after each direction] Tap your foot three times. Ready, go. Clap your hands once and then touch your nose once. Ready, go. Touch your head, touch your elbow. Ready, go. Stand up, sit down, and clap your hands two times. Ready, go.

Remind the children they must wait for the "ready, go" before proceeding.

Prepare a tape as follows:

You all have a colored block. When I call your color, do the things I tell you.

Red: Stand up, turn around, sit down. Ready, go.
Blue: Stamp your feet and nod your head. Ready, go.
Green: Stand up, jump two times, sit down. Ready go.
Yellow: Place your block on the floor, stand up, clap three times, sit down. Ready, go.
Blue: Stand up, hold your block high over your head, sit down. Ready, go.
Green: Hold your block behind your back and shake your head up and down. Ready, go.
Red: Place your block on your nose, then on your knee, then on your head. Ready, go.
Yellow: Stand up, sit down, walk around your chair, and sit down again. Ready, go.

Use a listening screen. One child gets on one side of a screen (a cardboard box opened up) with many different things to make sounds with, such as a bell, paper and scissors, water and a glass, and many more sound makers. Another child (or children) sits on the other side of the screen, where he tries to guess what makes the sound.

Use a flannelboard or a board with two hooks on it to classify the music heard on the tape recorder as fast or slow, happy or sad. Have four cards on the table with the tape recorder; one with a rabbit (fast) pictured on it, one with a turtle (slow), one with a happy face, and one with a sad face on it. When a selection of music is heard, the child (or children) operating the center picks up the two illustrations he feels best fits the mood of the music. Is it happy or sad? Is it fast or slow? About thirty seconds of each selection is enough time to let the students decide.

Play a tape of the *Nutcracker Suite,* the *Grand Canyon Suite,* the *William Tell Overture,* or other such selections. Provide crayons, paint, or chalk and paper for students to illustrate the things they hear in the music.

Make a center filled with things kids can make sounds with, such as bells, maracas, balloons, plastic or rubber tubing, sticks, shells, stethoscopes, and clocks.

Make a homemade ukulele with rubber bands stretched to nails in a board about a foot long. Put the nails at different intervals and use rubber bands of different widths to get different sounds.

Make an animal sounds center. One student gets behind the screen and one or more children listen on the other side as he makes noises like animals. They try to guess which animal they hear. A variation of this would be to construct a bingo game with animal pictures in the squares. When the child makes the animal noise on one side of the screen, the children on the other side can cover that animal if they have it on their card. The child making the noises would need some small cards with animal pictures on it to draw out of a box so the sounds would be randomly done and all animals included.

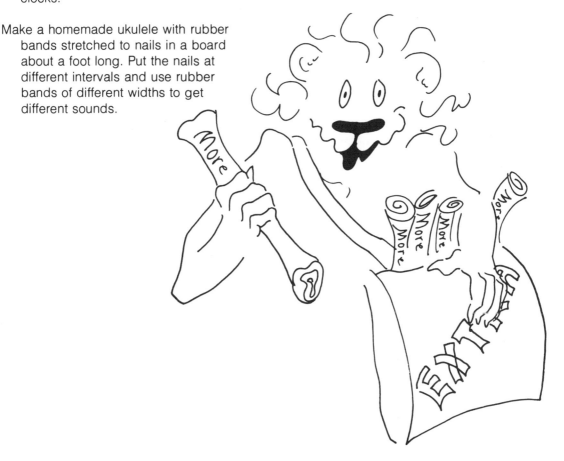

Use the plastic L'eggs containers for a listening center activity. Place dried beans in six of them—2 in one, 10 in one, about 25 in one, 40 in one, 55 in one, and 70 in one (approximate the number of beans). The child arranges the containers in order, from the one with the least to the one with the most. If this is too easy, make the numbers of beans in each one closer to the number of those in the one before. When the child is through arranging them, he can carefully open them up and either read a number inside that tells him how many are in the egg or count the number there.

Another way to use the same idea is to put the same number in two eggs with the task being to find the eggs that have the same amount in them. Two eggs could have five each in them, two might have fifteen each in them, and so on. The child must shake the eggs to determine which two have the same amount in them.

Make a listening center with eight water glasses filled with water at different levels. The children strike the glass with a spoon to make sounds. A tape or a worksheet could easily be worked up to go with this center. The glasses could also be numbered.

Put a different object in the "secret box" every day, or let children bring small items to put in it. The other children try to guess what is in it by its sound when they shake it. This game might lead to a twenty-questions-type game to guess what's in the box.

Play bouncing bingo. The children with cards know which number to cover by the number of bounces they hear (a marble in a can, a ball on the floor) on a tape recorder or from a child behind a screen.

Hide a loud ticking clock and let two children try to find it in the room by listening for its sound.

Have several children sit around in a circle and play add-a-word-to-the-story. The first child might say *once*, the second child *upon*, the third child *a*, the fourth child *time* to get the story started, then each child in turn would add a word to make the story continue. They must listen carefully to be able to add a word that makes sense.

Tape-record poems that lend themselves to interesting visual imagery. The children transfer what they hear to pictures in their minds. When the poem is over, the children in the center have a discussion about what they "saw" while listening to the poem. Paper and art supplies can illustrate the things they "saw."

Play "I'm Packing a Bag" or "I'm Taking a Trip." Vary these games to keep interest high. Sometimes you could be packing a bag and taking things that end in a *t* sound or a *p* sound. Other times you might take a trip and take with you things that begin with an S. The children play the game by taking turns naming something in accordance with the rule for that game. Another variation is to go through the alphabet; the first child packs something that begins with the letter A, the next child must pack something that begins with B, and so on through the alphabet.

Tape the following:

This is the story of "The Three Bears."
Listen for these three things:

1. What did the little girl do when she got to the house?
2. What did she do in the house?
3. How did the story end?—good or bad?

[read the story here]

Now, take a sheet of paper and some crayons. Fold the paper in half. On the front in one part of the paper draw a picture of what the little girl did when she got to the house. In the other part on the front draw a picture of how the story ended.

Options: The children can tell the story in correct sequence by a chart or by sequence cards. This idea can be used for stories not so familiar as "The Three Bears" and the tasks can be varied as the need arises.

Give each student an envelope containing five cards, each of which has a consonant printed on it. After you or a tape recorder or another child says a word, the student holds up the beginning consonant of that word.

Borrow real phones from the telephone company or use play phones for children to have conversations with others in the class. The center should be constructed so the children on the phones cannot see each other; thus, listening becomes all-important.

Use a record or a tape of a familiar story. Children should be given pictures of words that are heard in the story. When a student hears the word his picture depicts, he should hold it up.

Let pupils play and listen to different types of instruments. After they are familiar with them, have them close their eyes while the instrument is played (either on a tape or by a child in the center). They will try to guess which instrument has been played.

SPELLING CENTERS

Provide sheets of 9" x 12" colored construction paper, scissors, glue, and magazines. Children cut letters from magazines (or newspapers) and put them together to make each of their spelling words.

Make crossword puzzles using spelling words, or better yet, provide the necessary paper, rulers, and pens for children to make up the crossword puzzles.

Make a bingo game out of spelling words.

Get one envelope for each spelling word. In each envelope put all the letters necessary for one spelling word. Children choose an envelope and try to put the letters in the correct sequence. Try using an egg timer to race by. Using numbers, code the envelopes to a list of the spelling words so that a child who is stuck on a word can find out what the word is if necessary.

Provide a box of toothpicks and small cards with a spelling word written on each. Children duplicate the words on the cards by placing toothpicks over the letters on the cards. Then they form the letters off the card. They can also try making words of their own choosing.

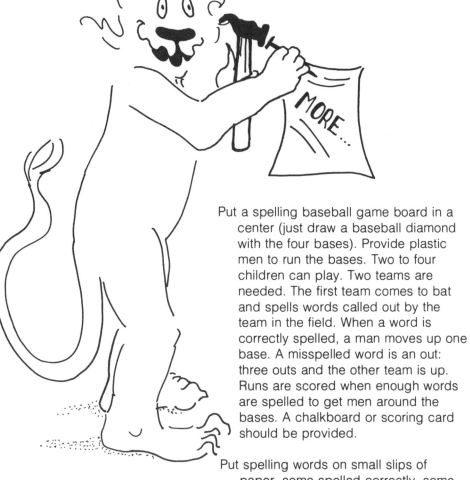

Put a spelling baseball game board in a center (just draw a baseball diamond with the four bases). Provide plastic men to run the bases. Two to four children can play. Two teams are needed. The first team comes to bat and spells words called out by the team in the field. When a word is correctly spelled, a man moves up one base. A misspelled word is an out: three outs and the other team is up. Runs are scored when enough words are spelled to get men around the bases. A chalkboard or scoring card should be provided.

Put spelling words on small slips of paper, some spelled correctly, some spelled incorrectly. Fold the small papers and put them in a container such as a can or box. Children work together; the first one draws a word, pronounces it, and spells it as it is on the paper. The other child tells whether it is the correct spelling or not. If it is not, he spells it correctly. A scoreboard can be devised to keep score of how many correct responses each makes. Then the other child draws a word and repeats the process to the first child who drew.

Place flannelboard (felt) letters in a center with a flannelboard. Children work in pairs, one calling out a spelling word and the other spelling it with flannelboard letters. The caller then checks the word. Partners change positions after about five words.

WRITING SKILLS CENTERS

Put out various things for children to manipulate. This develops the fine muscles they use in the writing process.

Examples of manipulative materials are:
ropes with knots to be untied (the child can then tie knots back in the rope for the next child to untie)
lacing cards
pegboards and pegs
Play-dough
- Popsicle sticks to build with
nuts and bolts to take apart, mix up, and get together again
various fasteners, such as things to zip, button, tie, snap, and lace

Let children practice letters or draw pictures on the chalkboard. A section can be marked off to contain a board assignment such as:
What children in our room have names that start with B?
What do you want for Christmas?
What do you like to eat?
Where would you like to visit?
How many words do you know that start with Wh?
Name some of your favorite toys.

Have children draw pictures with straight lines only, then write a story about it.

Have children make placemats to provide a real purpose for writing their names. The mats may be used at milk time or party time or may be taken home. They could also make them for the other members of their family.

Prepare laminated or contacted cards of the letters of the alphabet, leaving space for children to trace the letter. As in the illustration, draw lines resembling a first-grade writing tablet for children to write their own version of the letter. These cards can be wiped off for the next child.

For each child, prepare a newsprint page (use both sides) that has written on it the letters, numbers, or words he needs to practice writing. Provide clear plastic page protectors in the center that the child slips his newsprint page into and writes away. Because he can erase what he writes, he can practice it over and over. Store these prepared sheets in folders to be recalled at another time. Crayons, grease pencils, and washable markers can be used—the more colorful the better. Extend this idea to dot-to-dot pages, an old workbook you like but have only one or two copies of, and so on.

Buy a piece of plate glass any size you wish as long as it is larger than 8" x 10". Glue something on the four corners, such as a block or a round tinker toy, so that when it is turned over these "legs" will keep it above the table an inch or so. Slip underneath the glass any pages you wish children to practice writing. When they finish tracing, they remove the prepared sheet and the one they wrote. A piece of white poster paper underneath the whole thing makes their writing more visible.

Put cardboard letter patterns or stencils in the writing center for students to trace around. They could also take these to the chalkboard to trace them.

Don't forget,
integrate subject matter!

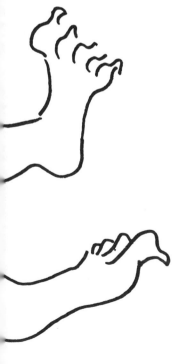

Chapter 3
In Mathematics

"2" begin with, learning centers in mathematics are "4" the teacher who wants to individualize instruction. "1" way to introduce a center in this particular discipline is to analyze the learning skills to be taught and to initiate centers that will self-teach them in a pleasant and meaningful manner. Once you get started, you will find it as easy as "1, 2, 3." Just review the samples shown in this segment and adapt them to your particular classroom needs. Note how mathematics centers can integrate other content into their structure through careful planning.

Focus in on Math

WHAT'S IT FOR?

To provide practice in basic computational skills.

STUFF YOU'LL NEED

- display board
- poster board
- markers
- glue
- tape
- scissors
- construction paper
- string
- games

HOW'S IT WORK?

The student may choose any activity to begin or may be directed to specific activities he needs.

1. *Math Messages*—Children complete activities on basic combinations in addition, subtraction, multiplication, or division.
2. *Square Up*—Puzzle pieces are fitted together to form a square.
3. *Land on the Moon*—Children play a game using basic combinations (any computational area) to go by steps to the moon.
4. *Fraction Jumbles*—Children match cards with different statements of equivalent fractions on them.
5. *Multiplication Football*—Children move down the football field by giving correct responses to basic multiplication questions.

HOW'D THEY DO?

Written work is placed in a hand-in box for teacher evaluation.
Individual conferences are held with pupils as they complete activities.

FIT'N IT IN

Have children apply basic computational skills in activities related to other curriculum areas.

Shape – O

Shape-O Picture Gallery

3.

Box of Shapes

Glue

Puzzles

4.

Box of Shapes for Mobile

5.

Directions

Shape-O-Toss

2.

WHAT'S IT FOR?

To enrich the understanding of geometric shapes (circle, square, rectangle, triangle).

STUFF YOU'LL NEED

- laminated construction paper
- laminated poster board
- colored construction paper
- glue
- ditto sheets
- bottle caps
- cardboard boxes
- grease pencil
- florist wire
- fabric
- dowel stick
- 1" x 6" board

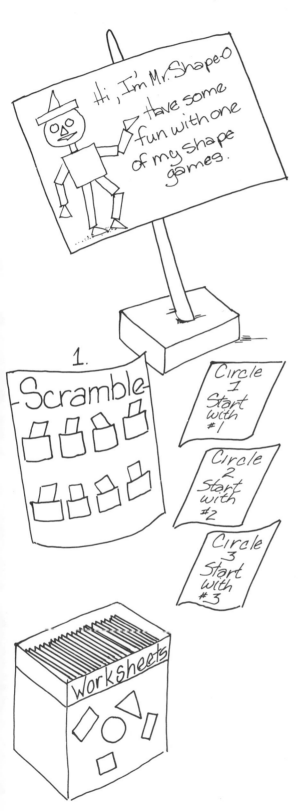

HOW'S IT WORK?

Children may complete activities in any sequence; however, worksheet activities may be a follow-up to manipulative activities.

1. *Shape Scramble*—Children take the letters provided and put them into sequence to spell the names of various shapes.
2. *Shape-O-Toss*—Children toss bean-bag onto box with the various shapes on it. The object is to identify the shape on which the bean-bag lands.
3. *Shape-O-Picture Gallery*—Children use provided shapes to create pictures, or they may make their own shapes.
4. *Shape Puzzles*—Children use puzzle pieces to build different geometric shapes.
5. *Shape Mobile*—Children use various shapes from the box to create geometric mobiles. Children may also create their own shapes for the mobile.
6. *Worksheets*—Children complete worksheets as needed.

HOW'D THEY DO?

Teacher checks ditto worksheets, views pictures made by students, and observes students during the toss game, spelling activity, mobile work, and puzzle solving.

FIT'N IT IN

Language Arts—Have children write stories about "Shape-O Pictures" or complete story starters ("A Day in the Life of a Triangle").

Social Studies—Let children visit various professionals who use geometry in working (carpenters, draftsmen).

Feel it, Guess it!

Work with a partner
puts on a
Turn around 3 times
find a number — it
what is it?

← blindfold

HOW'S IT WORK?

The sandpaper numerals are mounted around the edge of a table or are taped onto a chalk tray. Children work with a partner. One of the team is blindfolded and is turned around three times and pointed toward the sandpaper numerals. He feels a numeral and guesses from its shape what it is.

WHAT'S IT FOR?

To use a kinesthetic approach to help children identify numbers.

STUFF YOU'LL NEED

- numerals 1 through 10 cut from coarse sandpaper and mounted on poster paper
- blindfold
- direction sheet

HOW'D THEY DO?

Each child can list the numerals he identifies correctly.

FIT'N IT IN

This activity can also be used with letters of the alphabet and with shapes.

Pegboard Math

WHAT'S IT FOR?

To develop legible numeral formation.

STUFF YOU'LL NEED

- pegboards
- pegs
- ditto sheets with holes colored in patterns of numerals
- construction paper strips with numerals 1 to 10 written on them—one set for each child

HOW'S IT WORK?

On their pegboard children copy the pattern of colored holes on a ditto sheet posted in the center. They show it to an adult or older child, then punch a hole in their construction paper strip under the number whose design they just completed. No particular order is necessary. When every number on the strip is punched, they have completed the activity and place the strip in their math folder.

hole puncher →

HOW'D THEY DO?

An adult or older student checks the number designs as they are made. The child uses a hole punch to punch out numbers completed. The teacher can check math folders to see how many are working at this center.

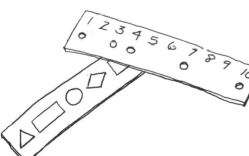

FIT'N IT IN

This activity can be done with the letters of the alphabet and with shapes such as triangles, circles, and squares, or any design that can be colored in on a ditto sheet for children to copy on peg boards.

Ladybug Math Center

WHAT'S IT FOR?

To develop skill in matching dots and pictures that represent the same number. To develop the concept of equal sets.

STUFF YOU'LL NEED

- poster board
- scissors
- pictures of objects
- glue
- red construction paper
- clothespins

HOW'S IT WORK?

Cut large circles from poster board and divide into six or eight sections (like a pie). In each section place a picture or drawing of objects. If the pie is divided into eight sections, one section should have a picture of one object, another should have a picture of two objects, and so on around the circle. Glue red construction paper ladybugs on one side of spring-type clothespins. The ladybugs have different amounts of dots on their backs to match the pictured objects on the circle. Provide enough paper ladybugs for each child to have one.

Children match the ladybug with two dots to the picture on the circle of two objects, the ladybug with seven dots to the picture of seven objects, and so on till the whole circle is filled. Each child who completes the center pins a paper ladybug on himself.

HOW'D THEY DO?

A quick glance around the room at who is wearing a ladybug will tell how many have visited the center. A comment such as, "Oh, Billy, I see your ladybug is crawling on your shoulder!" or "Jeannie, have you named your ladybug yet?" will encourage others to work at the center to earn their own pet ladybug.

FIT'N IT IN

Social Studies—match up community helpers to a tool or equipment they use.

Colors—use paint-store samples on the wheel and on the clothespins.

Shapes—match a shape on the wheel to clothespin that has same shape.

More Math—match up numerals and dots or numerals and pictures.

E–Z Money Corner

WHAT'S IT FOR?

To enforce money-counting and change-making concepts.

STUFF YOU'LL NEED

- poster boards
- envelopes
- laminated owls
- trains
- pockets for envelopes
- different coins
- paper play money

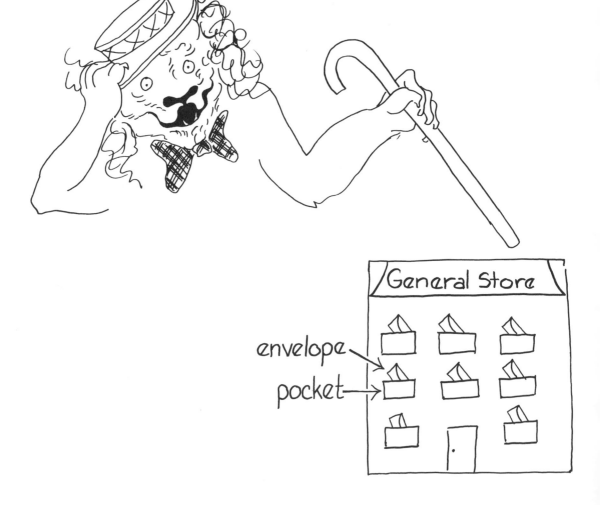

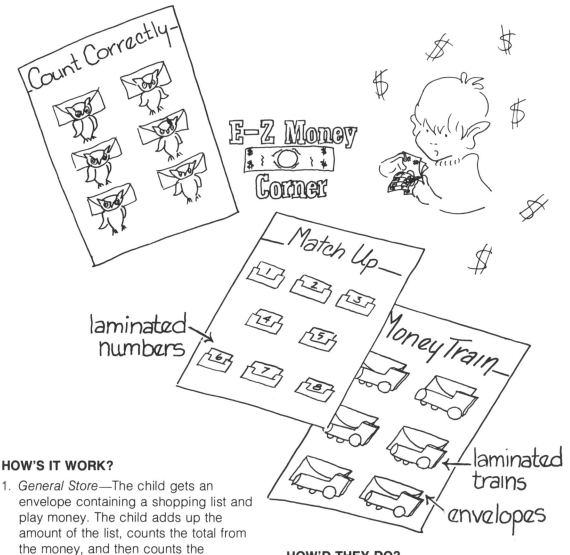

HOW'S IT WORK?

1. *General Store*—The child gets an envelope containing a shopping list and play money. The child adds up the amount of the list, counts the total from the money, and then counts the change.
2. *Money Train* Same procedure but with word problem in envelopes.
3. *Count Correctly*—Same procedure but with word problem in envelopes.
4. *Match Up*—One child calls out numbers. Underneath the number is an amount of money. A student reads the amount and at the same time tries to match two numbers with the same amount underneath (two players).

HOW'D THEY DO?

Students check their own answers with answer keys in folders

FIT'N IT IN

Language Arts—Children can write their own shopping lists and develop vocabulary skills while doing this math activity.

Geo-Fun

WHAT'S IT FOR?

To reinforce basic geometric concepts: shapes, solids, planes.

STUFF YOU'LL NEED

- construction paper
- typing paper
- markers
- pencils
- glue
- wood
- contact paper
- cardboard
- transparency film
- transparency frame
- rubber bands
- lined and ruled paper

HOW'S IT WORK?

1. Using the mobile as a guide, students create and label a picture.
2. Using the geo-solids, the students locate and list other objects in the room based on these solids.
3. Students construct geo-shapes on a geo-board.
4. Using the transparency with overlay, the student fills in the hand-out sheet on naming the parts of a geo-figure (vertex, base, etc.).
5. With yarn the student constructs a line segment, ray, line, curve, simple closed curve, and closed curve, using a guide.

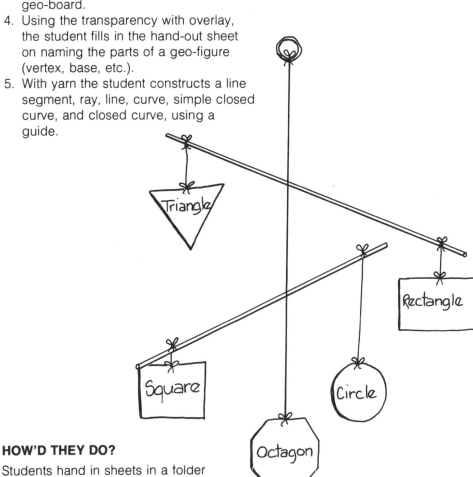

HOW'D THEY DO?

Students hand in sheets in a folder provided.

FIT'N IT IN

Creative Arts—Children can also create objects and identify their shapes with animals, food products, toys, and so on.

Ice Cream Addition

WHAT'S IT FOR?

To match pictures of equations to mathematical equations.

STUFF YOU'LL NEED

- construction paper
- marker
- index cards

HOW'S IT WORK?

Mount construction paper ice cream cones that have two dips—different flavors—on each cone. Each of the dips should have dots drawn on it. Contact or laminate if possible. Make a set of math equations that will match the dots on the cones (see illustration).

Children match the math equation on each card to an ice cream cone with that many dots. They read the equation aloud as they match it.

HOW'D THEY DO?

The cones can be numbered and a worksheet provided for children to copy the equations down as they match them up. Otherwise the only check is the completed match-ups.

FIT'N IT IN

Language Arts—An experience chart of words or pictures would be a natural development.

Science—Make ice cream.

What Makes What?

HOW'S IT WORK?

Use Cuisenaire rods or make your own by cutting 1″ x 1″ or 2″ x 2″ wood into lengths. It is also possible to make these rods out of poster board or construction paper and laminate or contact them. Children see what combination of rods will be as long as a 10 rod—(such as an 8 rod and a 2 rod). They record their combinations and put them in their math folders.

HOW'D THEY DO?

Check children's work as they go along in the center. Evaluate combinations to see if children exhausted the possibilities or did just enough to get by.

FIT'N IT IN

Creative Arts—Design creative structures with the Cuisenaire rods.

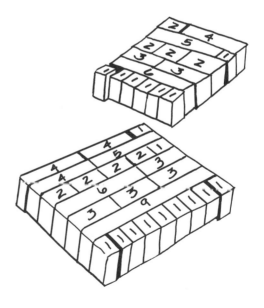

WHAT'S IT FOR?

To provide children with experience with concrete objects.
To explore math concepts.
To experiment with lengths of objects equal to other lengths.
To develop mastery of basic addition combinations.

STUFF YOU'LL NEED

• Cuisenaire rods
• paper

The Big Board

WHAT'S IT FOR?

To develop children's awareness of number patterns.
To practice counting by 2's, 5's, and 10's.
To develop the concept of what comes before or after a number.

STUFF YOU'LL NEED

- colored construction paper (ten different colors)
- large board
- 100 hooks, nails, or pins
- cards
- marker

HOW'S IT WORK?

Make the big board by placing nails or hooks in ten rows of ten. Make cards for numbers 1 to 100, and color code them vertically so that 1, 11, 21, and so on are the same color, 2, 22, 32, and so on are the same color, etc.

Children put number cards on the big board in order. They see how many directions—up, down, sideways, etc.—they can count numbers in some kind of order or pattern. They can count by 2's, 5's, and 10's. Take some of the numbers off the board and mix them up—children put them back in the right spot. A worksheet can be included at the center to teach a specific task. Children should be encouraged to discover number patterns and to tell everyone about them.

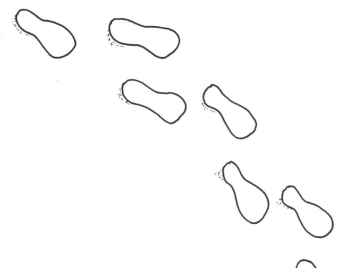

on the floor in front of the board!

HOW'D THEY DO?

If a worksheet is prepared, it can be checked for progress and discoveries children make. The best evaluation will be what a child does at the big board. Teacher observation.

FIT'N IT IN

Social Studies—Programming can be developed via the playing of bingo and cards.

Silly Sulushuns!

WHAT'S IT FOR?

To reinforce fraction concepts.
To give children concrete experience with fractions.

STUFF YOU'LL NEED

- felt pieces
- flash cards
- graph paper
- crayons
- mimeographed sheets
- scissors
- nuts and bolts
- display board
- construction and poster paper
- magic markers
- tape
- glue

HOW'S IT WORK?

Children may choose activities to complete at random or may be directed to specific activities they need.

1. *Fancy Fractions*—Children manipulate felt pieces to determine equivalent fractions.
2. *Meet Mr. Common D. Nominator*—Child chooses a card with three fractions on it and gives a common denominator for them. He continues until he misses.
3. *Square Fractions*—Child colors on graph paper to show a specific number of hundredths.
4. *Ring Around*—Children circle the smallest and largest in each row of fractions on a mimeographed sheet.
5. *Nuts and Bolts*—Children place a nut with a fraction on it onto a bolt that has an equivalent fraction on it. Nuts only fit bolts that have equivalent fractions on them.

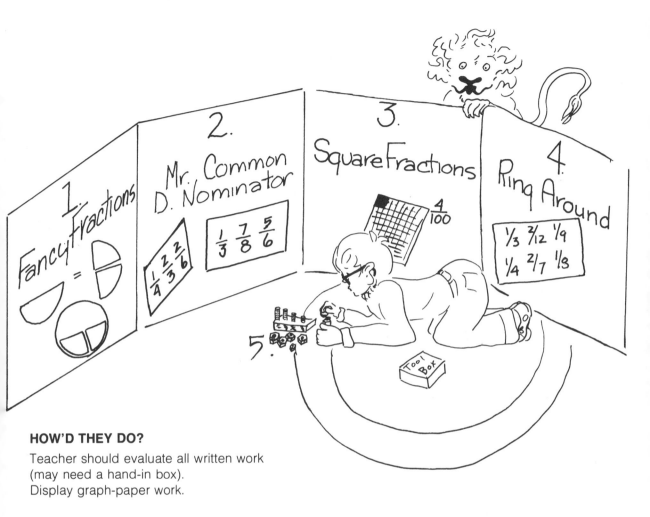

HOW'D THEY DO?

Teacher should evaluate all written work
(may need a hand-in box).
Display graph-paper work.

FIT'N IT IN

Language Arts—Have children write story
    problems using concepts of fractions:
    Write fraction poetry and fraction
    riddles, or write, role-play, or tell a
    real-life experience in which knowing
    concepts of fractions is necessary.
Social Studies—Have persons from various
    professions (such as a baker or
    seamstress) tell the importance of
    knowing concepts of fractions.
Art—Have children illustrate fractional
    equivalents using a variety of media.

more ideas
in Math Centers

Put together an ordering kit. Use three or four different sizes of each of the following items: paper sacks, juice cans, buttons, paper cups, towel rolls (cut to different lengths), rubber bands, pencils, washers, baby food jars with different amounts of beans in them, blocks, straws (cut to different lengths). Children order each set from largest to smallest or most to least. Store them in a box.

Make a bingo card set with numbers or math facts for children to play with.

Make a game box and fill it with teacher- and children-made games.
Examples:
Raceway
Use dice and matchbox cars to see who wins the race. If you land on a shaded space, go back two spaces.
Willie the Worm
Use dice and markers to see who can get to the end of Willie first.

Glue pictures of sets of objects on poster paper. In the center draw a numeral. Children use construction paper squares to cover all the sets on the board that depict a number other than the written one.

Put numerals on 1″ x 1″ blocks and place them in a plastic bowl or bucket. Children ladle out a bunch of numerals and place them in sequential order. Or, instead of numerals, use fractions to be ordered.

Cut large numerals out of sandpaper sheets and mount them on colorful poster paper squares to be put up in the math center. Provide a blindfold for children to wear with instructions for them to name as many numbers as they can by feeling them.

Buy and laminate dot-to-dot sheets for the math center.

Cut up old calendars into small squares, each square with a number from one to twelve. Place the squares in an envelope. Children choose an envelope and arrange the numbers in sequence, left to right.

Make geo-boards with an 8″ x 8″ board and headless nails. Nail twelve or sixteen nails in rows of four, leaving ¾″ or 1″ of the nail above the board. Provide rubber bands of all sizes and colors for children to make shapes with or to cover a certain amount of nails.

Make giant dominoes for your math center. Cut wood to desired size—4″ x 5″ is good. Paint the wood blocks black. When they are dry, drop white paint onto the blocks to make dots. Use a strip of white adhesive tape for the center dividing line. Shellac over all.

Glue four paper plates together to make one sturdy paper plate. Make as many of these thick paper plates as you need to make match-up boards. Divide the paper plate into pie slices—about six or eight on each plate. Put a numeral or shape or dots in each wedge section. Provide clothespins with numerals, shapes, dots, addition facts, or colors, which can be clipped to the wedges that they match.

Put a measuring box in your math center. Fill it with measuring devices such as a tape measure, ruler, 6-inch ruler, sewing gauge, folding yardstick, and others. Children measure tables, chalkboards, and other equipment and spaces in the room.

Use plastic photograph cubes for a match-up activity. In the sections of one put dots of different amounts. In another cube put numerals, pictures, or math facts that can be matched to the other cube. Children turn the cubes until they find the matches and record them on a worksheet.

Secure carpet samples and spray-paint numerals on them. Children can use the hall or classroom to put them in order or to put the even numbers in order or the odd numbers. Another effective way to use carpet squares is to cut them into giant footsteps and spray numerals on them.

Make a game with butter tubs. Cover the tops of four to six tubs with a circle of contact paper. Inside each tub put paper squares with numbers 1 through 10, or as high as you wish. Each player has a tub. When it is his turn, he draws a numbered square. After each player has drawn a number, the person with the highest number gets to keep all the drawn numbers. He places them in his tub and everyone draws again. Whenever the players want to end the game, they simply count their squares and the winner is the child with the most in his tub.

Cut animal shapes or flower shapes out of colorful poster paper. Draw a numeral in the middle of each one. After covering them with contact paper, place them and a pile of paper clips in the center. Children clip the same number of paper clips on the poster paper as the numeral on it.

Play concentration. A board may be used for sixteen cards or twenty-five cards (in which case the center card holds the name of the game). It has many possibilities: matching colors and shapes, addition problems, subtraction, multiplication, fractions, and so on. The child who makes the most matches wins the game.

Cover three squares of cardboard with small pictures of toys and groups of toys (from catalogs or magazines), and put clear self-adhesive paper over them. Make many tiny tiles, which are placed face down. Each player turns over one tile at a time. If he has a set of toys on his board to match the number, he places the tile on that set. If he has no matching set, the player replaces the tile, and the next player chooses. The game is over when one player covers his board.

Give children this problem: Place the figures 1, 2, 3, 4, 5, 6, 7, 8, 9 in a 3″ x 3″ grid so that the sums across, down, and diagonally will equal 15.

EXPERIMENTS WITH MEASUREMENT

Encourage the children to experiment with noncalibrated measuring cups. Have them fill small cups with water and observe how many are needed to fill a larger cup and whether anything remains. From this activity proceed with calibrated measures. Lead the children to see the need for standard measuring devices. Use this recipe to make clay for use by the children:

    1 cup salt
    2 cups flour
    ¼ cup salad oil
    1 cup water
    food coloring or dry tempera paint

Ask the students: "Suppose we were to use just any cups to make the recipe? Would the results be the same if we changed back and forth, using different cups?"

Make copies of the following problems or ask them as questions:

1. How many red stripes are there on the flag?
   How many of them are white?
   How many stripes in all?
2. There used to be forty-eight stars on the flag. There are fifty stars on the flag now. How many more stars were put on?
3. How many stripes are there in all on the flag?
   Are the stripes all the same length? There are six long stripes. How many of them are short?

Make large cards with things in the first column that match things in the second column. Use shoestrings to match things that go together. (Put knots in one end of the shoestring and bring it up through a hole next to the items in the first column. Then make a hole near the items in the second column for the shoestring to go into.)

Draw five toys at the top of the board or paper and under each toy write its price. Under this write several questions about the toys in the "store." Children may answer either by filling in a numerical answer in a blank or by putting "yes" or "no" at the end of the sentence.

1. The ball and top together cost _____.
2. The car costs _____ more than the kite.
3. Does the kite cost more than the top? _____.
4. The jacks, top, and kite together cost _____.
5. Do the jacks cost less than the car? _____.
6. The kite costs _____ less than the car.

Prepare sixteen 2-inch squares with numbers and number combinations on them. The child puts the squares together so that the sides that are touching name the same number. 1 and 2 could touch a side that has 3 on it, and so on.

Make a large board with three columns, one for numerals, one for number names, and one for dots. Each column should have ten hooks going down. Make fish with numerals, number names, and dots on them and put a paper clip on the nose of each fish. Using a fishing pole with a magnet on the end, children "catch" the fish and place them on the board according to which row they belong in. Color coding the rows might be helpful. For example, all the fish with numerals on them might be green, all the number-name fish might be blue, and all the fish with dots might be yellow.

Put fish with numbers representing their weight in the center of a table. The student draws from a pile of directional cards that tell him to pick up two fish whose total weight equals a certain amount. He records this math problem on a worksheet and draws another card. Be inventive with the directional cards. Some could have dots or pictures or a number of objects for children to match a fish with.

Inside a fish bowl place paper fish with sets of pictures to be added or subtracted. Children fish, and if they give the correct answer they may keep the fish. The child with the most fish at the end of the game wins.

Make bowling pins out of tall orange juice cans with numbers on the sides. Place in usual bowling rows. Use Nerf ball or yarn ball. When children bowl they record the numbers they knock down and add them together each time to get their score. The child with the highest score is the winner.

Tell children they are detectives and they must investigate some missing numbers. They read the description cards for the missing numbers, then list the number of the description card and the number they believe is missing.
Examples of description cards:
Attention all detectives. We have a missing number. He is even. He has an older sister who is four. Can you identify him? (2)
Attention all detectives. A number is missing. It was last seen around the middle of the number line. It has five 10s, is odd, and is smaller than 53. Who is it? (51)
Attention! The bank has just been robbed. The robber got one dime, three nickels, and two pennies. How much money is missing? (27 cents)

Remember,
integrate subject matter!

Chapter 4
In Science

Science is a discipline that should be learned via direct experimentation. Learning centers can help the individual teacher provide such experiences for children in the classroom environment.

Many times learning centers from other discipline areas (language arts, science, mathematics, social studies, creative arts) can be integrated into science education. The main thing is to get children involved in the learning process. The centers shown in this chapter should excite your five senses and make you and the students begin to experiment in the classroom.

Underwater Experiment

WHAT'S IT FOR?

To show that air has weight and takes up space and will push water away.
To get children to think about why this experiment results as it does.

STUFF YOU'LL NEED

- directions poster
- clear plastic glass or jar
- stack of paper towels
- water in pan or pail about 3 or 4 inches deep

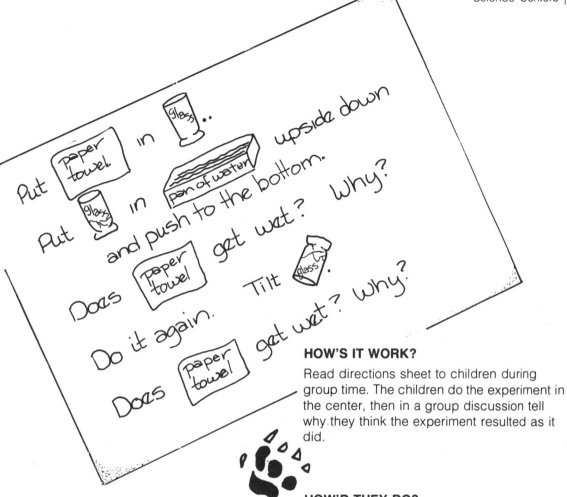

Put paper towel in glass..

Put glass in pan of water upside down and push to the bottom.

Does paper towel get wet? Why?

Do it again. Tilt glass. Why?

Does paper towel get wet? Why?

HOW'S IT WORK?

Read directions sheet to children during group time. The children do the experiment in the center, then in a group discussion tell why they think the experiment resulted as it did.

HOW'D THEY DO?

Evaluate children's thought process in reaching conclusions in a group discussion.
Did children of all abilities attempt to answer why?
Was there enough structure to the center so that children knew what to do?

FIT'N IT IN

Language Arts—Children record their work by drawing pictures of the results as indicated in the illustration.
Math—Children can count the number of steps involved.

Will it float?

WHAT'S IT FOR?

To provide experiences for further development of concepts of space and weight.

To get children to form conclusions about what kinds of materials do and do not float.

STUFF YOU'LL NEED

- two plastic tubs half-filled with water
- bottle tops
- squares of construction paper
- squares of aluminum foil
- sponges
- cotton balls
- Popsicle sticks
- jar tops
- pencils
- worksheets
- tape recorder

HOW'S IT WORK?

The first two days set up the center with a sign that says, "Will it float? Make a list." Provide a worksheet that allows students to classify a variety of items as to whether they float, do not float, or float and then sink. Students draw a picture or write the name of the item in the proper column. During these two days children simply try out all the items, discovering which will and which will not float.

On the third day, add a tape recorder, with a tape that says:

When you put something into the water, it pushes some of the water away. If it weighs more than the water it pushes away, it sinks to the bottom. Put a pencil into the water. (pause) Does it sink? (pause) Yes, because it weighs more than the water it pushed away. If something is flat its weight is over a large area and it floats better. Put the square of aluminum foil into the water. (pause) It floats nicely, doesn't it? Now crumple the tin foil into a small ball and place it into the water. Does it float or sink? (pause) Yes, it sinks because all the weight is in one little ball. Some things float at first but then sink when water seeps in and makes them heavier. Put a piece of cotton into the water. It floats for a second, then as it fills up with water it sinks. Take a worksheet and answer the three questions.

Children listen to the tape while performing the experiments they are directed to do. Upon completion of the tape, they answer the following three questions on a worksheet:

1. If something weighs more than the water it pushes away, it (sinks, floats).
2. Why does the flat aluminum foil float but the ball of foil sink?
3. Some things float at first but then sink when _____.

HOW'D THEY DO?

Check the worksheets the children have filled in.

FIT'N IT IN

Language Arts—By dictation or by writing, children can record the results of their experiments.

Math—Counting techniques can be included in the various activities.

Temperature Takers

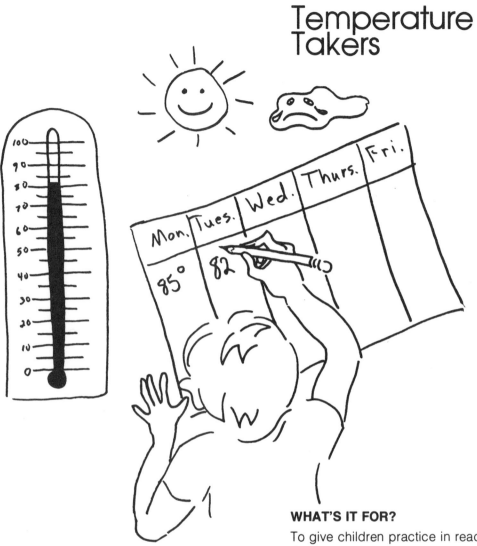

WHAT'S IT FOR?

To give children practice in reading a thermometer.
To compare and contrast outside and inside temperatures and temperatures on different days.

STUFF YOU'LL NEED

- two thermometers
- poster board
- manila envelope
- worksheet

HOW'S IT WORK?

Hang a thermometer inside the classroom at children's eye level away from heater and sun. Hang another thermometer outside the classroom with face in view through a window. Make a large poster board kangaroo with a large manila envelope for a pocket. Write directions on the envelope for students to make a record of indoor and outdoor temperatures for each day. Children keep track of temperatures for a week and then complete a worksheet with the following questions:

1. What was the highest inside temperature?
2. What was the lowest inside temperature?
3. What was the highest outside temperature?
4. What was the lowest outside temperature?
5. Did it get colder or warmer outside as the week went along?
6. Is it mostly warmer inside or outside?

HOW'D THEY DO?

Check every day to be sure children are recording temperatures. Provide older student or adult help, especially for those who cannot write their answers on a worksheet by themselves.
Did answers to questions show any needs for further learning in this area?

FIT'N IT IN

Language Arts—Children learn abbreviations for days of the week. Adapt this activity for a writing lesson.

Math—Ask children to list temperatures in order, from high to low, and to find the average temperature. They could also subtract high temperatures from low and inside temperatures from those outside.

Vibrations

WHAT'S IT FOR?

To hear and create vibrations.

STUFF YOU'LL NEED

- fork
- piano (optional)
- tissue paper
- tin-can telephone (string tied between the bottoms of two cans)
- other materials with which children can invent ways of making vibrations, such as rubber bands

HOW'S IT WORK?

Give directions in group time. Children should pick a partner, then use the materials in the center to make vibrations. Directions might include:

1. Strike the fork on a hard surface and put it near your partner's ear.
2. Play a note on the piano while your partner's ear is flat against the side.
3. Sing into the tissue paper.
4. Stretch the tin-can telephone string tight and talk to your partner. Take turns touching the string lightly.

HOW'D THEY DO?

Evaluate in a group session what learnings and concepts of vibrations were gained.

FIT'N IT IN

Music—Let children listen to different notes on the piano with their ear on one side and then tell whether a note is higher or lower than the preceding one.

Make a ukelele with rubber bands stretched over nails on a board.

Language Arts—Children write a story of what the first telephone conversation might have been like.

Art—Children draw what they think vibrations in the air would look like if they could see them.

Balancing

HOW'S IT WORK?

Children manipulate different kinds of balancing materials to see what balances what. There is no worksheet or structure or task at this time. Children are encouraged to discover what happens if the board on the log is moved off center. How can it be balanced? Children are encouraged to work together.

HOW'D THEY DO?

Evaluate this center by observing participation and enjoyment and by class discussion: what happened when . . .

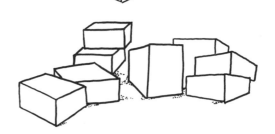

WHAT'S IT FOR?

To learn to distribute weight evenly so that balance is attained.

STUFF YOU'LL NEED

- balancing scales
- 1" x 6" board, 3 to 4 feet long
- 6" to 10" section of a log with bark removed and a flat side cut
- long strips of cardboard, paneling, and other lightweight woods for balancing
- blocks of all sizes, shapes, and weights
- set of uniform colored blocks that children can use in order to discover that two reds balance a blue, and so on

FIT'N IT IN

Math—Mark blocks with numbers. Have some 1's, 2's, 3's, 4's, one 5, one 6, and so on through ten. How many 1's balance a 4? How many 3's balance a 9?

Language Arts—Use new vocabulary such as fulcrum, balance, and so on in spelling and stories.

Magic Magnets

WHAT'S IT FOR?

To give children an opportunity to see what a magnet will do.
To provide children with practice in following directions for carrying out experiments and reporting results.

STUFF YOU'LL NEED

- direction sheet
- shoe box
- man and dog stand-up puppets
- paper-cup house
- plastic tub with sand and paper clips mixed together
- plastic pan with water and small boats floating in it
- a dozen paper clips
- several strong magnets
- pocket for "Dear Magic Magnet" letters

HOW'S IT WORK?

Set up the center on a table or the floor. Children choose one of the four activities and follow directions in completing it. After they have done all four activities (over several days if they wish) they write or dictate a "Dear Magic Magnet" letter, which lists the things they have discovered the magnet will do. The letter is placed in a designated spot.

1. A shoe-box stage is turned on one of its long sides. A man and dog are moved around on stage by placing magnets under them. The paper clip on their stand will be attracted and will move as the magnet under the "stage" moves. It would be useful to demonstrate this activity in a group time, making the dog chase the man and the man chase the dog into the paper-cup house, and so on.
2. Provide a plastic tub of sand with paper clips all mixed in. Children move the magnet through the sand, picking up the paper clips as it goes.
3. Provide a pan of shallow water with little light-weight boats (with paper clips on the masts or sails) floating in it. Children draw the magnet slowly above boats to make them sail.
4. Provide a dozen paper clips and a strong magnet. Children place as many clips end to end as the magnet will hold.

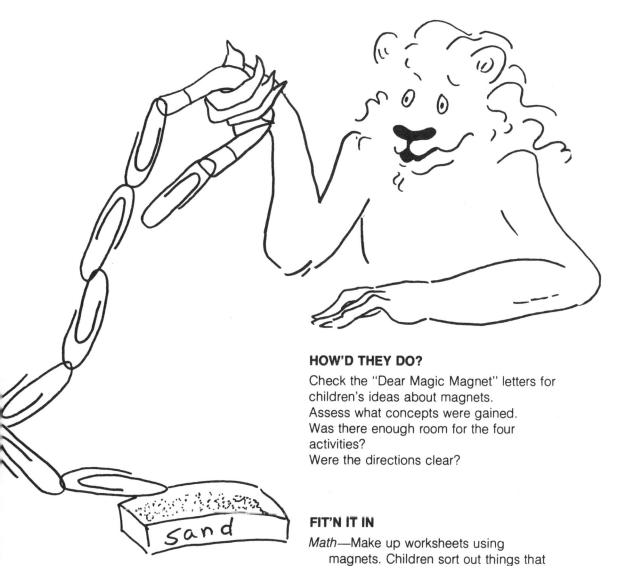

HOW'D THEY DO?

Check the "Dear Magic Magnet" letters for children's ideas about magnets.
Assess what concepts were gained.
Was there enough room for the four activities?
Were the directions clear?

FIT'N IT IN

Math—Make up worksheets using magnets. Children sort out things that are and are not attracted by the magnet.

Social Studies—Using magnetic puppets, put on a puppet show about the current social studies unit.

Is something **bugging** you?

WHAT'S IT FOR?

To create interest in the study of insects.
To develop understanding of insect
development.
To compare and contrast insects and man.

STUFF YOU'LL NEED

- jars
- lids
- cotton
- alcohol
- dowels
- coat hangers
- netting
- filmstrip
- projector
- honeycomb
- pictures of bees and honeycomb
- tagboard or poster paper
- markers
- reference books

HOW'S IT WORK?

Activities may be completed in any sequence children choose.

1. Children construct a killing jar for collecting insects.
2. Children construct an insect net for collecting insects.
3. Children view a filmstrip on insects and how they live.
4. Children observe a honeycomb and reference pictures, and answer questions about the honeycomb.
5. Children (working in groups of four) prepare a chart comparing the way bees live and work together with the way humans live and work.

HOW'D THEY DO?

Examine insect collections.
Provide an answer box for written work.
Groups present their charts.

FIT'N IT IN

Language Arts—Use "insect" words in vocabulary study. Assign creative writing involving such things as, "I woke up and found myself in the middle of a giant beehive."

Math—Have children figure the proportionate weights a man could lift if he were as strong as an ant. Speeds of various insects could be used in distance/time–type problems.

Art—Build a "man-sized" honeycomb from cardboard.

Real Spacy!

WHAT'S IT FOR?

To create curiosity about outer space.
To develop the concept of space travel.
To provide opportunity for creative thought
in science.

STUFF YOU'LL NEED

- filmstrip and projector
- task cards or poster
- books
- record and player
- tape and player/recorder
- study prints
- several sets of sequenced space-flight
  pictures

HOW'D THEY DO?

Teacher observes students and evaluates written work. Other students provide feedback.

FIT'N IT IN

Math—Various computational activities can center on distances and speeds in space flight. Have children build a scale model (using a mathematical scale) of the solar system. Have children build bar graphs showing size and speed of various rockets used in launchings.

Language Arts—Incorporate "spacey" words into vocabulary study, spelling, and phonics activities. Gear creative writing and dramatic activities in space-flight and exploration themes. For example: "Pantomime a man walking on the moon," or write a story that begins, "All of a sudden my capsule went into an antigravitational counter-orbital spin and I . . ."

Social Studies—Have children locate space-flight centers and tracking stations on maps. Explore space exploration costs and needs for problems here on Earth.

HOW'S IT WORK?

Activities may be completed in any sequence.

1. Children view a filmstrip on the solar system and then answer specific questions (place questions on task cards or poster paper).
2. Children examine books on space. Each chooses a book to read and share (a guidesheet may be provided).
3. Children listen to a record of a space flight, then answer questions concerning the flight.
4. Children listen to a tape of their capsule crash-landing on the moon. Then they turn over the tape and report what they observe on the moon. The tape can be played back for a friend to check.
5. Children choose a study print and write three things they know about what they see.
6. Children (in a group of three to five) arrange a set of pictures into correct sequence (blast-off to landing). Then they write a group story about the sequence of events.

Eco-Crisis

WHAT'S IT FOR?

To develop sensitivity to problems of pollution.

STUFF YOU'LL NEED

- reference books
- crossword puzzle
- cassette recorder
- tape
- filmstrip
- projector
- study prints
- collage backing
- glue

HOW'S IT WORK?

Children may work on any activity without concern for sequence.

1. The child locates ecology vocabulary words in provided references and completes the crossword puzzle.
2. The child utilizes a filmstrip and tape on pollution to answer questions concerning causes of pollution.
3. Study prints are examined to determine solutions to problems posed on task cards.
4. Children build a collage using litter collected and brought to school.

HOW'D THEY DO?

The teacher examines the crossword puzzles, question answers, and tasks.

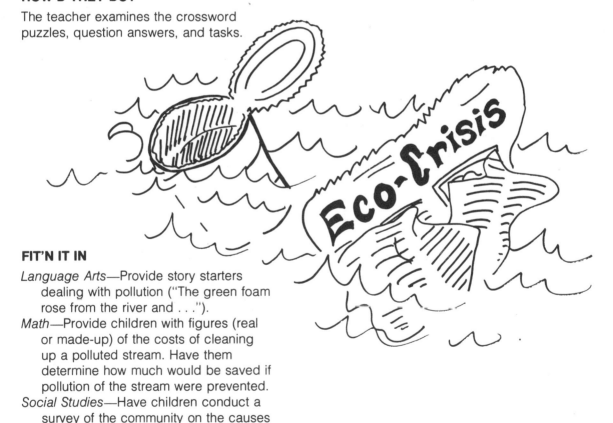

FIT'N IT IN

Language Arts—Provide story starters dealing with pollution ("The green foam rose from the river and . . .").

Math—Provide children with figures (real or made-up) of the costs of cleaning up a polluted stream. Have them determine how much would be saved if pollution of the stream were prevented.

Social Studies—Have children conduct a survey of the community on the causes of pollution.

more ideas
in Science Centers

Grow some mold! Put a piece of wet paper in a glass jar. Place a piece of bread on top of the paper and let it stand for a day or so in a dark place. Mold will form and children can view it under a magnifying glass.

Provide magnifying glasses in the center for each child to actually view his own skin. He can describe what he sees and draw it. Further studies on the uses and importance of skin can also be presented.

Write on white paper with a clean pen dipped in lemon juice. When the lemon juice dries, the writing will be invisible, but press it with a hot iron and the writing reappears.

Do a center on simple machines. Look for machines used in the home and around school. Provide wheels, incline planes, pulleys, and other simple machines that kids can mess around with. Slide a box of blocks across the floor. Then put the box on wheels. How do the wheels help? Try to pull a load up some steps, then use a ramp. Why is it easier?

Have students explore "fullness." Fill a jar or glass with marbles. Is it full? Put sand in the glass. Is there room? Is the glass full now? Is there space for some water? When is the glass full?

Put a lid on an empty jar. Float it in a pan of water. Fill the jar with water. It sinks. Compare the weight of air to water.

Comb your hair rapidly on a cool, dry day. Then hold the comb near small pieces of paper. Talk about how the electricity draws the paper.

Place colored water in a clear jar. Put a stalk of celery or a daffodil with a long stem in the water. Let children observe what happens to the celery and flower.

Put sand, salt, and sugar in the science center, with instructions to mix a tablespoon of each in separate glasses of water. Which dissolves? Which does not?

Instructions to students:

Set up a center on evaporation. Wet your hands, and shake them until they are dry. Where did the water go? Put a wet handprint on the chalkboard and see how long it takes to evaporate. Fan some handprints and not others. Which evaporate first? Put one wet cloth on a heater or in the sun and another in the shade. Which evaporates first? Put a small dish of water in the sun and one in the shade. Which evaporates first?

Grow winter greenery. Cut carrots about one inch from the top, and place the tops in a shallow dish of water. Green leaves will grow. Place a medium-size onion in a small amount of water in a plastic butter tub. The children will delight in seeing a green stem grow from the top. Birdseed or rye grass seed sprinkled on a wet sponge in a pie pan will germinate quickly and stay green for a long time. A small amount of water should be kept around the sponge. Place the end of a large sweet potato in water in a clear glass jar or vase. Children will enjoy watching for the roots to grow and for green vines to appear.

Set up a center on liquids and solids. Use containers of water, milk, syrup, cooking oil, and similar liquids. Also provide solids such as blocks, rocks, crayons, soft drink bottles, jars, and ice. Ask students: Which are solids? Which are liquids? Which liquids are thick? Which are thin? Are all solids hard? Are all solids the same shape? Will solids fit in all kinds of containers? Will liquids? What shape do liquids become when they are poured into a container? Can we make water, a liquid, into a solid?

Talk about living things. Arrange a display of living and nonliving things. Children can sort and build exhibits of their own with explanations of their collection.

Show that plants need air, light, and water. Display a plant that gets all three. Cover one plant so that no light gets in but so that it does get air and water. What happens to it? Put another in a bigger jar and put the top on to shut out all air, but give it light and water. What happens to it? Give another plant air and light but no water. What happens to it?

Collect flowers for the science center. Take a flower apart. Look at the petals, pollen tubes, tiny seeds, stem, and so on under the magnifying glass.

Put water in a plastic or other nonmagnetic bowl. Make a toy boat out of something that floats, such as a small piece of wood, floating soap, a walnut shell, or a piece of cork. Use a nail or steel pin to attach a small sail made out of a scrap of material. Your children can move the boat across the water without touching it by moving the magnet in the direction they wish the boat to go.

Explain to the children that earthworms are found in topsoil. Tell them that they can observe how earthworms look in the soil. Put some topsoil and earthworms in a jar. Cover the jar with black paper. The next day have children open the paper and look in. They should be able to see the worms making tunnels.

Take tomato soup and cook it for a few
minutes to free it of any germs. Then,
after it's cooled a little, pour a small
amount into containers on which each
child has labeled his name. Each child
can either cough in the soup, sneeze,
put a finger in, put a hair in, or
whatever. Cover the containers tightly
and let stand four days. Children can
watch the bacteria grow and have
discussions.

Place a list of animals and a list of places
where they live on the board. Let the
children come to the board and draw
lines from the name of the animal to
the place where they think it lives.
Example:

bird	underground
fox	water
fish	jungle
rabbit	grass
lion	nest
alligator	den
mole	swamp

Set up an incubator and chick eggs.
Children keep a running tabulation of
data—temperature, days before
hatching, process of hatching, weight
of chicks, descriptions, and so on.

Have one box labeled "Yes" and one
labeled "No." Children put things that
a magnet will pick up in the "Yes" box
and others in the "No" box. Then they
can talk about what the things in each
box have in common.

Make a box to represent each floor of
Noah's Ark. The boxes should be
labeled "Zoo," "Wild," "Pets," and
"Farm." Give children pictures of
animals that would fit in these
categories and ask them to help Noah
divide the animals.

Are you integrating subject matter?

Chapter 5
In Social Studies

Working cooperatively is one of the major skills to be learned
if a student is going to effectively deal with his social environment. Learning
centers can naturally provide experiences that will promote these valuable
social skills. In addition, the learning can be geared to meet varied student
abilities without social or intellectual stigma attached. Being able to gear
instruction at the level desired also promotes social understanding and
positive attitudes toward all members of the world community.
The social studies learning centers in this section will provide the teacher
with a starter kit. Once started, you will find that you can create even
better centers all by yourself.

What do you know about Saudi Arabia?

WHAT'S IT FOR?

To introduce and develop knowledge about Saudi Arabia.

STUFF YOU'LL NEED

- information on Saudi Arabia
- globe
- worry beads
- filmstrip on Saudi Arabia
- various Arabian materials
- art supplies

HOW'S IT WORK?

The child may choose any activity to begin.

1. *Drilling for Oil*—Children read and discuss information about oil wells and oil rigs.
2. *Look!*—Children look at a filmstrip describing the religion, climate, and geography of Saudi Arabia.
3. *Where Is Saudi Arabia?*—Children use a globe to determine the size, location, and boundaries of Saudi Arabia.
4. *The Worry Corner*—Using Arabian worry beads, the children write stories about what Arabians might worry about.
5. *Oil Country Problems*—Children complete math problems related to pipelines, oil production, and costs.
6. *Arabian Art*—Using reference-book pictures of Arabian art, the children describe, in writing or in pictures, their ideas about life in Arabia.

HOW'D THEY DO?

The teacher observes the children and holds individual conferences.
Writing and art should be displayed.
Self and peer checking is used in globe and math activities.

FIT'N IT IN

Language Arts—Children write stories with Arabian themes.
Math—Computation may center around the oil industry.
Art—Children produce artwork depicting Arabian life.

Hawaiian Islands I.D.

WHAT'S IT FOR?

To develop recognition of the number of islands in the Hawaiian chain and their names.

To develop size and location relationships between islands.

To develop ability to spell words associated with the Hawaiian Islands.

STUFF YOU'LL NEED

- large board painted sea-blue with Hawaiian Islands outlined on it
- clay models of each island
- flag with name of each island on it
- picture cards of: pineapple, outrigger, volcano, lei, hula, grass hut, coconut palm, orchid, conch shell
- phrase card describing item depicted
- word card for each item

HOW'S IT WORK?

1. The child uses the blue board with outlines of each island drawn on it to put models of each island in its correct location. Then he places the correct name flag for each island on the correct island.
2. The island of Oahu is marked with a red star. The child is to determine why the star is there and to indicate his reason (the capital, Honolulu, is located on Oahu).
3. The child takes the picture cards and the phrase cards provided and matches them. Then he spells the word on a notepad that goes with each picture and phrase.

HOW'D THEY DO?

The child checks his own work on each activity with an answer key that is provided.

FIT'N IT IN

Math—Children compute distances between the islands and the areas of the islands. Give consideration to map-reading skills.
Science—A unit may center around formation of islands, volcanoes, tidal waves, and so on.
Art and Music—Provide experiences with Hawaiian art and music.

Our Community Helpers

WHAT'S IT FOR?

To develop recognition of community helpers.
To develop skill in identifying jobs of community helpers.
To encourage creative expression.

STUFF YOU'LL NEED

- tape recorders
- blank tapes
- record/filmstrip on community helpers
- study prints of community helpers
- flannelboard and cutouts
- cards with pictures of helpers and equipment glued to them

HOW'S IT WORK?

The child may choose any or all of the following activities.

1. *Stop, Look, and Listen*—Children play the record/filmstrip titled *Neighborhood Friends and Helpers*.
2. *A Story! A Story!*—Children look at a set of community helper study prints and tape stories about what they see.
3. *Mix and Match*—Children play a card game in which they try to match community helpers with the equipment they use in their jobs.
4. *Do Your Thing!*—Children place a flannel cutout of the helper described on a tape up on the flannelboard, or they may draw or paint their favorite helper.

HOW'D THEY DO?

Listen to taped stories.
The flannelboard activity is checked by comparing numbers on backs of cutouts with number given on the tape.

FIT'N IT IN

Math—Children count the number of helpers described on the tape. Older children could add up amounts of monies paid to community helpers.

Language Arts—Use community helper words for spelling list and reading vocabulary words. Develop creative dramatics activities around community helpers.

Comparisons!

WHAT'S IT FOR?

To develop ability to compare two distant but similar geographical regions.
To develop understanding of different types of manufacturing.

STUFF YOU'LL NEED

- globe and string
- large box and several small boxes
- several story starters
- tape recorder and tape
- art materials
- game board, die, and game pieces

HOW'S IT WORK?

1. *As the Crow Flies*—Using a globe and its scale, the child measures (with a string) the distance between Pittsburgh and Bombay.

2. *Surprise!*—The child reaches into a large box and draws out a smaller box, which contains a vocabulary list, a beginning sentence, a beginning paragraph, a picture, or a story title. The child then writes a story.

3. *India*—Children listen to a taped Indian folk tale and then draw pictures illustrating it.

4. *Treasure Hunt*—Children play a game that uses a game board upon which statements about either Pittsburgh or Bombay have been written in each movement space. At his turn, the child throws the die, moves to a space, and indicates whether the statement refers to Pittsburgh or Bombay. If he is correct, he stays there. If wrong, he goes back to his original space.

HOW'D THEY DO?

Writing is to be turned in to the teacher. The game is self-checking.

FIT'N IT IN

Language Arts—Special words may be included in spelling and reading vocabulary.

Math—Children compute travel time at different speeds from Pittsburgh to Bombay. They may also compute cost of a trip, or figure and compare wages and salaries of workers in India and the United States.

Can you weave?

WHAT'S IT FOR?

To experience the activities involved in weaving textiles.
To foster creativity.

STUFF YOU'LL NEED

- shoe box
- yarn
- wood frame (picture frame)
- jute (burlap)
- rugpunch needle
- rubber latex cement

HOW'S IT WORK?

1. *Box Weaving*—Make a box with slits ½ inch deep and ½ inch apart in the opposite sides. The child strings yarn across the top of the box, passing the yarn through each slit twice. Then yarn is woven under one string and over the next string until the top of the box is covered. The weaving can be used as a wall hanging, place mat, or whatever.

2. *Rug Weaving*—A simple design is drawn on a piece of jute strung on a wood frame. A rugpunch needle is then threaded and punched in and out along the drawing, using about five stitches per inch. After the outline is complete, it is filled in with other stitching in other colors. When complete, the rug is removed from the frame. The back and edges of the rug can be secured with rubber latex cement.

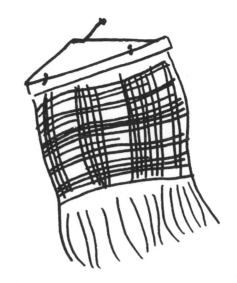

HOW'D THEY DO?

Activity should be evaluated in personal terms (individual beauty, neatness, creativity).
Work skills (cooperation, active involvement) may be observed.

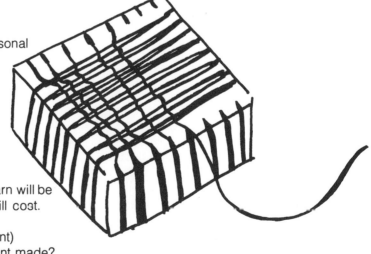

FIT'N IT IN

Math—Children figure how much yarn will be needed or how much material will cost.
Science—Why does weaving stay together? How does glue (cement) work? How is rubber latex cement made?
Language Arts—Utilize words from the textiles industry for spelling list or for vocabulary in reading. Creative writing could be developed around rug and weaving patterns.

How did you get to school today?

WHAT'S IT FOR?

To make children aware of their routes of travel in the community.
To familiarize them with the overall layout of the community.

STUFF YOU'LL NEED

- poster paper
- contact paper
- small cars
- crayons

HOW'S IT WORK?

Make a map of the main streets in the community, including each child's street and the school. Make it on large poster paper or cardboard and cover it with contact paper. Let children help put their names on the street where they live with crayon.

Children trace their routes to school, first with the toy cars then with a crayon line. Then they use the cars to show how they could get to town, a shopping center, church, or the grocery. The only line drawn is the one from their house to school.

HOW'D THEY DO?

An older child or adult can guide all the children to participate by checking whose name has a line from home to school. Use the finished map in a group discussion about who has the longest or shortest distance to travel, and so on.

FIT'N IT IN

Math—Count the blocks to school or let children find out how many miles they ride to school in a day and add to find out how many they ride in a week.
Language Arts—Children write a story about an adventure they had on the way to school.

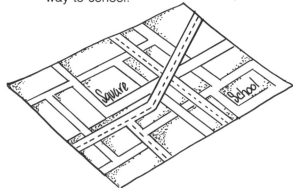

Community Helper Riddles

HOW'S IT WORK?

Children read the riddles on a poster and solve them by putting a picture of the correct helper in a pocket by the riddle. Upon completion of all the riddles, the child uses an answer sheet to check his work. The children autograph a fireman's hat or put a note in a mailman's bag with their name on it when they are finished in order to know who has been to the center.

WHAT'S IT FOR?

To reemphasize the jobs people do.
To have fun answering riddles.

HOW'D THEY DO?

Check on how many children have used the center. Does it need to run several days? For children who don't read, could picture riddles be put on the poster paper for them?

STUFF YOU'LL NEED

- poster paper
- envelopes
- pictures of community helpers

FIT'N IT IN

Math—Use math riddles.
Science—Have riddles about animals, insects, magnets, and so forth.

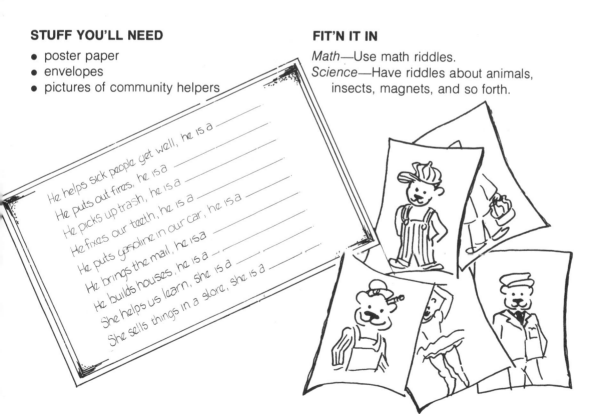

He helps sick people get well, he is a ———
He puts out fires, he is a ———
He picks up trash, he is a ———
He fixes our teeth, he is a ———
He puts gasoline in our car, he is a ———
He brings the mail, he is a ———
He builds houses, he is a ———
She helps us learn, she is a ———
She sells things in a store, she is a ———

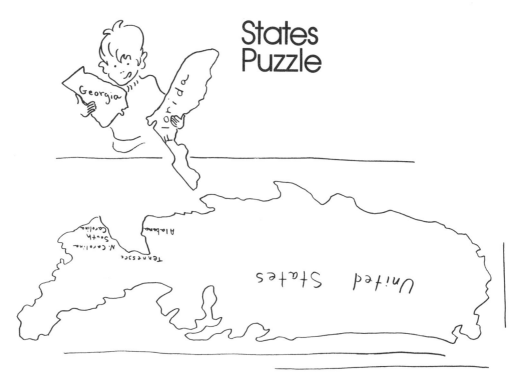

States Puzzle

WHAT'S IT FOR?

To learn where one's state is in relation to others.

STUFF YOU'LL NEED

- opaque projector
- map of United States
- contact paper
- scissors
- crayons

HOW'S IT WORK?

Using an opaque projector, enlarge a U.S. map to large poster-paper size. Cut it out and cover with contact paper. Use crayons to fill in names of each state. Cut out the state you live in along with four to eight others bordering on it or close by. Children put states back into place in the whole map (they will fit in like a puzzle), as they name each one. After children have had some experience with the map, erase states' names and see whether they can name them.

HOW'D THEY DO?

Hand out a ditto sheet of your states area and have children fill in or tell orally what the states' names are. Is this activity too difficult for some who really want to do it? Can it be simplified?

FIT'N IT IN

Language Arts—Children can learn to spell names of states.
Math—Children can count all states, putting a crayon mark on them as they go.
Science—Use the map to do a geography lesson.

Community Helpers Talk to Us

HOW'S IT WORK?

Make masks of five community helpers—for example, a doctor, a policeman, a dentist, a fireman, and a postman. Make them on poster paper at least as large as a child's head and glue or staple a tongue depressor to each one so that it may be held in front of the face. A good way to make these is to find a small picture of the helper and enlarge it on an opaque projector and then cut it out.

Children take turns in the center pretending to be the helper whose mask they hold. They give safety rules or health rules and generally tell things a real helper would say if he could talk to the children in person.

HOW'D THEY DO?

Children might want to have a dialogue with the five community helpers in front of the whole class. Did most children participate in this center activity? Was there adequate time for children to explore it fully?

WHAT'S IT FOR?

To dramatize what children imagine community helpers would say to them.

STUFF YOU'LL NEED

- poster paper
- markers
- glue
- tongue depressors
- opaque projector

FIT'N IT IN

Art—Children could make the masks as an art project.

Science—This same activity could be done with masks of animals and/or insects. Children might tell what animal or insect they are and something about it.

This is my house!

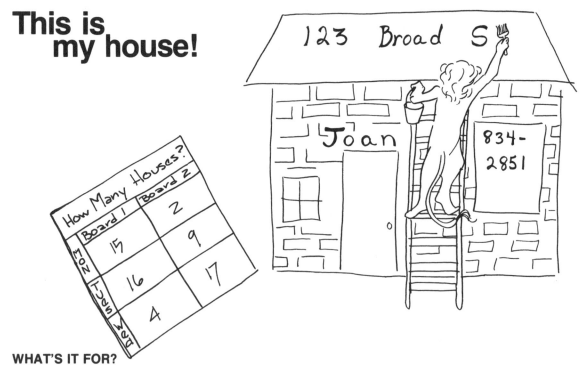

WHAT'S IT FOR?

To learn addresses and phone numbers.

STUFF YOU'LL NEED

- white, brown, yellow, red, and green construction paper
- scissors
- crayons
- Magic Markers
- tape or pins

HOW'S IT WORK?

Children draw a picture of their house (use white for white frame, red for brick, or whatever color the child's house is). An adult in the classroom, or the child if he can write, puts the address on the roof and the telephone number on a window. The child then tapes or pins his completed house in a designated place.

HOW'D THEY DO?

To check who has used this center simply see whose house is missing from the display. When the child memorizes his address and phone number, he takes his house home or displays it in another designated area.

FIT'N IT IN

Art—Constructing the house could be done as an art project.

Math—Children could keep a chart of how many houses are in the first display area and how many are in the second area. Children could be asked to add everyone's phone numbers together to see whose is the most and least.

Riding Through Georgia

WHAT'S IT FOR?

To familiarize children with main cities in their state.

STUFF YOU'LL NEED

- a road map of the state mounted on poster paper and covered with contact paper
- small cars to drive on roads
- ditto sheet or adult for oral report

RIDING THROUGH GEORGIA
I went to these cities:
1. _____
2. _____
3. _____
4. _____
5. _____
The longest trip was between
_____ and _____
The shortest trip was from
_____ to _____
The city nearest the
Ocean is _____
The city nearest Florida
is _____
The northern most city
is _____

Sample ditto sheet

HOW'S IT WORK?

Children use cars to travel on a map of the highways between the big cities of a state. (Put a crayon mark around the names of the five or six largest cities.) After they have explored around with it awhile, they work alone or with a friend to fill in the answers on the ditto sheet and place it in their file folder.

HOW'D THEY DO?

Check the ditto sheet for results of the center.

FIT'N IT IN

Math—Older children can do math with the road map, computing actual miles between cities by using a table prepared from the map by the teacher or students.
Language Arts—Children can learn to spell names of large cities in their state.

Japanese Jamboree

WHAT'S IT FOR?

To stimulate interest in study of Japan.

STUFF YOU'LL NEED

- film on Japan
- projector
- tape recorder and prepared tape
- word cards
- travel guides for Japan
- study prints and pictures

HOW'S IT WORK?

Children may choose to begin with any activity.

1. Children view the film, *Japan—Yesterday and Today,* and make a list of questions about things they would like to learn.
2. Children turn on a tape recording of Japanese-English language translation and listen. They then try to match word cards of English and Japanese words.
3. Children use various travel guides provided to plan a trip to, and a tour of, Japan.
4. Using various study prints and pictures of Japan, children write stories about Japan.

HOW'D THEY DO?

Teacher observes activities and holds individual conferences.

Peer- and self-checking are used in the word activity.

Creative writing and tour planning should be turned in.

FIT'N IT IN

Math—Tour planning should involve figuring costs. Also, have children convert United States currency to Japanese and reverse.

Language Arts—Incorporate the spelling of Japanese words into the spelling of English words.

Creative Arts—Let children perform Japanese ceremonial dances and drama.

more ideas
In Social Studies Centers

Place several pictures of community
helpers in a center and have children
take turns picking one without showing
it to anyone else. They must
pantomime the actions of the helper
until the other children at the center
guess which helper it is.

Make a center involving signs seen around the neighborhood, such as STOP, YIELD, RAILROAD CROSSING, SLOW, SCHOOL, NO PASSING.

When studying a part of the U.S. or a particular people such as Indians, fix the center up with books, artifacts, pictures, a typical village, and other interesting things for children to explore and manipulate.

Use a globe or world map to show the natural habitat of animals you are studying.

Put viewmasters and slides on social studies units in a center.

I said,
integrate the
subject matter!

Chapter 6
In Creative Arts

The creative arts have been organized in an integrated manner for years.
Art, music, and physical (movement) education lend themselves to this approach. You
can hardly do one without being involved in one of the other areas. Learning
centers can easily be organized to include art and music, or music and movement,
or art and movement, or all three. The centers shown in this chapter are simple
examples that can be built upon to form more complex creative experiences.
It might also be useful to integrate centers in mathematics, social studies,
and language arts with the creative arts. Just let your creative talents flow.
The results could be spectacular!

Indoor Bowling

WHAT'S IT FOR?

To enjoy playing a game while improving eye-hand coordination and sportsmanship.

STUFF YOU'LL NEED

- ten orange juice cans
- wallpaper, colorful contact paper, or paint
- Nerf ball

HOW'S IT WORK?

Paint orange juice cans or cover them with wallpaper or contact paper. Number cans from 1 to 10.
Place cans in bowling pattern on the floor. Children take turns rolling a Nerf ball to knock over the cans. Rules should be discussed beforehand.

HOW'D THEY DO?

Did children take turns and otherwise follow rules? Could adjustments in rules eliminate problems with the game?

FIT'N IT IN

Math—Children can record the numbers of the cans they knock down and make addition problems with them.

Home Builders Center

HOW'S IT WORK?

Children decorate the outside and inside of a box with their choice of wallpaper, carpet, and linoleum. They can make furniture from the blocks, spools, boxes, material scraps, and construction paper.

HOW'D THEY DO?

Provide a place for children to display their finished houses and give them the opportunity to explain their creations and ask questions about each other's work.

FIT'N IT IN

Social Studies—Use this for building materials or houses in the community. Use the activity to teach children their address and phone number. Study what furniture goes in what room.

WHAT'S IT FOR?

To provide children with an opportunity to design their own house, then use a variety of materials to make it.

STUFF YOU'LL NEED

- boxes—one for each child at least 12" x 18" or larger
- wallpaper books
- scraps of linoleum and carpet
- construction paper
- material scraps
- spools of all sizes
- small boxes
- blocks from building sites
- glue

Balance Beam

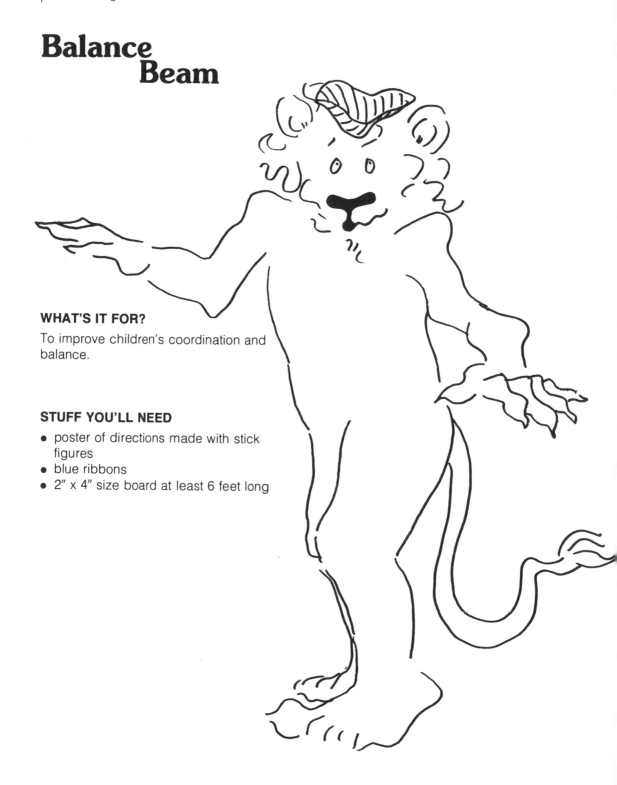

WHAT'S IT FOR?

To improve children's coordination and balance.

STUFF YOU'LL NEED

- poster of directions made with stick figures
- blue ribbons
- 2″ x 4″ size board at least 6 feet long

HOW'S IT WORK?

Children go down the directional poster doing the tasks on the balance beam. After they have completed the whole list they get to pin on a blue ribbon that has some inscription on it, such as Balance Beam Walker or Balance Beam Expert.

Walk across beam...
Walk with hands on hips...
Walk with hands up...
Walk with arms folded...
Walk with beanbag on each shoulder...
Walk with beanbag on your head...
Walk with beanbag on back of each hand...

Expert

HOW'D THEY DO?

Children who need extra time and help should be encouraged to keep trying the tasks until they complete them all, even if they do them in installments. All children should eventually get a ribbon.

FIT'N IT IN

Math—This is an excellent way of introducing measurement concepts to children while they enjoy body movement activities.

Tracing Fun

WHAT'S IT FOR?

To strengthen small muscles for control in writing.
To develop eye-hand coordination in writing.
To practice following a specific pattern.

STUFF YOU'LL NEED

- cardboard letters, numbers, and patterns
- newsprint
- markers, crayons, and pencils
- display poster

HOW'S IT WORK?

Children choose letters and patterns and fill up a large piece of newsprint with tracings. They can make their names, the alphabet, math problems, and many more designs. The tracings can overlap. Provide a place in the center for displaying finished products. (Children may wish to color the designs.)

HOW'D THEY DO?

By looking at pictures it is possible to tell which children have good motor control and which need more practice. Did children find it fun? Were kids creative?

FIT'N IT IN

Math—Children can do math problems by tracing numerals in problem form. Provide mathematical signs to trace around.

Social Studies—Patterns of community helpers or other social studies unit subjects could be traced.

Holidays—Patterns from various holidays can be traced.

Farmyard Fun

WHAT'S IT FOR?

To make a barn and animals to play with.

STUFF YOU'LL NEED

- boxes
- red paint
- construction paper
- crayons
- stapler

HOW'S IT WORK?

Children paint a box red (or whatever color they wish). The teacher cuts a barn door, hayloft, and windows. Children make animals out of construction paper to go in the barn. An easy way to make animals is to use an arch cut on the fold for the animals' body and legs. The child then cuts a head and tail and glues them on. Spots can also be added.

HOW'D THEY DO?

Teacher observes how children work together, share materials, and make joint decisions. Observe childrens' ability to use paint brushes, scissors, and to fold paper.

FIT'N IT IN

Drama—Children could role-play the farmer or the animals.

Science—Children study how the farmer takes care of the animals.

Social Studies—Examine the importance of farms, crops, and animals.

Math—Children could count the number of animals, and so on.

Impossible Animals

Girelephiger

HOW'S IT WORK?

Children draw around and cut out the animals they choose. They cut them apart so they have a head, body and tail, and legs—they select a head of one animal, a body of another, and glue them onto the newsprint. Children make up names for their new animals.

WHAT'S IT FOR?

To use imagination to combine parts of different animals to make a new one.

STUFF YOU'LL NEED

- patterns of giraffe, elephant, tiger, camel, lion, etc.
- construction paper of all colors
- scissors
- glue
- newsprint pages

HOW'D THEY DO?

Did children find this activity enjoyable? Was it easy enough to make up a new name?
Would it help younger children if the animals were already cut out and cut apart?

FIT'N IT IN

Science—Use this activity in a study of zoo or farm animals.

Making Musical Instruments

WHAT'S IT FOR?

To give children the opportunity to make their own rhythm instruments.

STUFF YOU'LL NEED

- orange juice cans
- dried beans and peas
- paper plates
- wire
- bottle tops
- masking tape
- L'eggs
- buttons
- shortening cans or oatmeal boxes
- construction paper
- crayons
- glue
- little Christmas bells

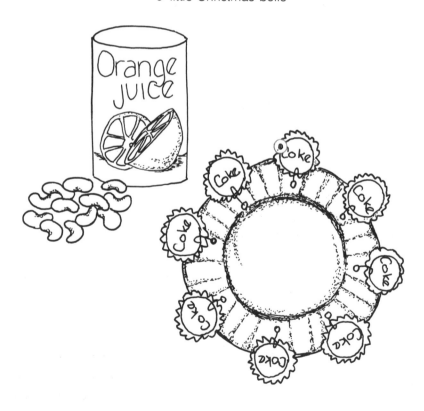

HOW'S IT WORK?

Children are shown three teacher-made instruments—a shaker made from an orange juice can with dried beans inside, a paper plate tambourine made with bottle tops wired to paper plates, and a drum made with an oatmeal box or decorated shortening can.

All these instruments are decorated with construction paper and crayons. Children are challenged to make an instrument of their own—either following the general pattern of the teacher-made instrument or making one of their own invention.

HOW'D THEY DO?

Check on who needs help by having an adult or older child posted at this center. Give help only if asked for. How many children ventured into new designs? Was music provided to play new instruments by?

FIT'N IT IN

Language Arts—Work on developing simple songs via use of finger plays, poems, and so on.

Say it, Play it
music center

WHAT'S IT FOR?

To judge whether music is fast or slow, happy or sad.

STUFF YOU'LL NEED

- tape recording of ten to twelve different musical selections (about 45 seconds of each selection)
- tape recorder
- four pictures or drawings each of a turtle, a rabbit, a happy face, and a sad face, all drawn or mounted on 4" x 6" cards with a hole in the top middle for hanging or with flannel on back for placing on a flannelboard
- flannelboard or board with hooks

HOW'S IT WORK?

Place all turtles, rabbits, happy faces, and sad faces in the middle of the table alongside the tape recorder. Children listen to selections on the tape and decide whether the music is fast or slow, happy or sad. They place a turtle on their board if they feel the music is slow, a rabbit if it is fast, and so on. They can compare what they thought about the music, then put back the cards to get ready to judge the next selection.

HOW'D THEY DO?

Children's participation is the best judge of this center. Was interest high? Was it O.K. to disagree?

FIT'N IT IN

Math—A piano or other instrument could play a certain number of beats or notes on the tape. Children put a card with that numeral up on their board.
Social Studies—Play sounds of community helpers at work. Children put up pictures of the correct one.

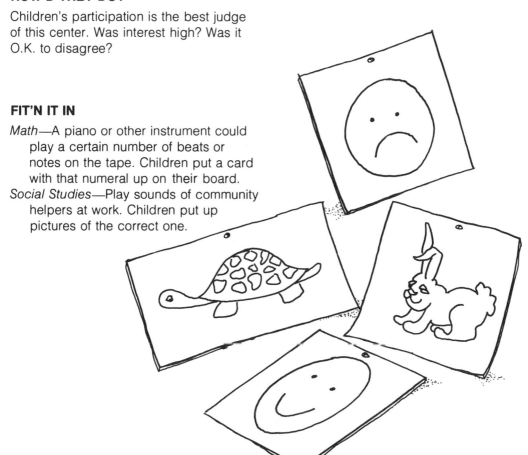

more ideas
in Creative Arts Centers

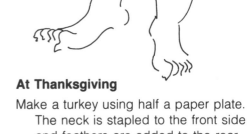

When Studying Indians

Make totem poles from paper towel rolls.
Children cut out eyes, noses, ears, and
mouths to put on their individual poles.
Or make one large class totem pole
using a carpet roll.

Make a teepee from construction paper.
Decorate it with Indian signs.

Make an Indian canoe and decorate it.

Make an Indian poncho from a 2- or
3-foot square of white sheet. Children
put on decorations with colored Magic
Markers, then add fringe around the
bottom.

Make Indian headdresses from a construction
paper band and feathers.

Make a bracelet from upholstery scraps
and leather-look material. It can be cut
in a long narrow rectangle and
punched along both long sides with a
hole puncher. Weave yarn in and out
both sides and use it to tie onto an arm.

Make Indian tom-toms from oatmeal boxes
or decorated shortening cans.

Make a clay pot.

At Thanksgiving

Make a turkey using half a paper plate.
The neck is stapled to the front side
and feathers are added to the rear.

Have children draw around their hand.
The thumb is the turkey's head and
the other fingers are tail feathers. Add
features and color.

Make a turkey pine cone. Place the cone
on its side and put a construction
paper head in front and tail feathers in
back.

Make pilgrim collars, cuffs, and hats for
children to wear.

Cut things from magazines. Each child
makes a book, *What I Am Thankful For.*

For Christmas

Make ornaments of different shapes out of construction paper and decorate them with crayons, glitter, rick-rack, lace, gummed reinforcements, and stars.

Make red and green chains to decorate the tree or room.

Make Rudolph the Red-Nosed Reindeer. Glue the bottom half of a large brown triangle onto a piece of green construction paper. Fold down the top half for Rudolph's face. Add eyes, nose, and glitter around his neck. For antlers cut Q-tips in half and glue onto construction paper.

Make a wreath. Cut the inside out of a paper plate and glue sections of egg carton around the circle. Glue wads of red and green crepe paper alternately in egg cups. Glue on a red crepe paper bow.

In Winter

Cut snowflakes from folded circles.

Use white crayons or chalk on dark paper to make snowmen and snow pictures.

Draw an outdoor scene. Use cotton for snow.

Mold a snowman from Ivory Soap Flakes—3 cups flakes to ½ cup water.

Make snowmen from styrofoam balls. Make a hat and broom and arms from toothpicks. Make a scarf from a scrap of cloth.

In February

Provide paint, construction paper, and crayons. Children choose one or more mediums to draw a log cabin like the one Abraham Lincoln was born in. Provide wooden sticks for children to actually build a log cabin.

Make three-cornered hats for George Washington's Birthday. Challenge children to draw a scene showing the legendary cutting of the cherry tree.

Teach children how to cut valentines on the fold of the paper or provide patterns in cardboard of all sizes of hearts. Challenge children to make a person entirely of hearts.

Make a table decoration or gift for parents out of an orange juice can covered or painted. Put clay or Play-dough in the bottom and insert pipe cleaners decorated at the top with leaves and heart-shaped flowers.

Cut hearts to make Valentine flowers on green stems.

Draw the trunk of a tree and the main branches. Cover with small hearts for the leaves.

Make Valentine hats by covering a band with all kinds of hearts.

Make Valentine bags by decorating white bags with hearts.

Music Centers

Tape music for children to draw by.

Put music stories in centers for children to listen to with earphones.

Put out a variety of musical instruments —such as song bells, autoharps, harmonicas, song flutes, guitars, and ukuleles—in the music center for children to strum and tweet on.

Physical Education Centers

Make a hopscotch on the floor for children to use.

Put knots in ropes. Children must untie them, then put more knots in for the next child to untie.

Make a maze out of a center for children to crawl or walk through.

General Ideas

Make gingerbread boys. Put out patterns for children to trace and cut out. Let them decorate with buttons for eyes, nose, and mouth.

Put a box of round things on the art table. Children can fill a page or a book of stapled pages with things that are round. Try other shapes, too.

Put a lot of construction paper squares, circles, triangles, and rectangles on the art table. Children arrange a design on newsprint and glue it down. Challenge them to make a man, wagon, house, or animal. There's nothing wrong with a pleasing design that's nothing in particular either.

Using the shapes mentioned above, make a bird with a yellow bill to go along with learning the poem "The Birdie with the Yellow Bill."

Cut sponges into 1- or 2-inch squares. Let children dab them into tempera paint and blot them on newspaper. They should fill a page with about three different colors of sponge blots. Fall leaves cut from these sponge pictures are beautiful. Children can draw a trunk first, then fill in branches of the tree with sponge blots.

Let children make a bird in flight when talking about migration.

Using one long half of an egg carton make a caterpillar. Paint dots on him, as well as eyes, nose, and mouth. Use pipe cleaners for legs and antennae.

Press some leaves in magazine pages. Put them on the art table with newsprint and crayons but without any paper. Children make crayon rubbings by placing leaves underneath newsprint and rubbing them with the side of a crayon.

In March

Make kites out of open sacks with yarn tied on each side of the open end. Decorate it. When the child pulls it, wind will fill the sack, causing it to "fly."

Make a pinwheel of construction paper on a straw.

Make a wind chime. Collect bells, bottle caps, and metal lids to put on a string and hang in the wind.

Using cardboard patterns, make shamrock rubbings with newsprint.

At Easter

Use L'eggs for making decorated eggs.

Make Easter chicks. Use a yellow circle for the body, a smaller circle for the head, and toothpicks for legs.

Cut an egg shape on the fold to make an Easter card that will open. Decorate it. Put a verse inside and have children sign it for their parents.

Make easy-to-hold Easter baskets out of gallon milk bottles. Add eyes, nose, mouth, whiskers, and ears from construction paper, and place a little grass inside.

Make Easter rabbits with construction paper and cotton.

In April

Make a "Spring Things Mobile." Put out patterns or challenge children to draw and cut out spring things, such as rabbits, turtles, kites, and ducks. Hang with yarn on a mobile made of a strip of poster paper stapled in a circle.

Use four strings of yarn tied to the top section to hang it up by. Punch holes around the bottom to tie spring things onto.

Challenge children to draw ducks and wet weather pictures.

Mark off mural paper into garden plots. Each child "plants" a garden on the paper by first coloring in the dirt (brown crayon with no paper wrapper, turned on its side), and then adding vegetables such as carrots, radishes, corn, pumpkins, watermelons, and beans.

Make cute animals by gluing a head on one end of a spool and a tail on the other end.

For Halloween

Tear ghosts out of white construction paper and add eyes and a howling mouth.

Make masks by decorating a box that will fit on a child's head with cut-out eyes, mouth, ears, nose, and other features.

Have children draw a scene with crayon on newsprint, bearing down hard so a lot of wax is on the paper. Using a thin wash of black tempera, draw a paintbrush back and forth over the picture. The heavy crayon marks resist the paint, and the completed picture will look like a night scene.

Make jack-o-lanterns with orange construction paper. Children can decorate them with black triangles of crayon or construction paper.

INTEGRATE THE SUBJECT MATTER!

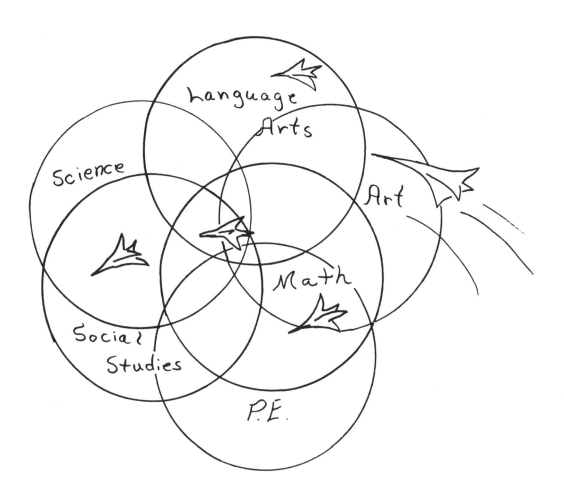

Chapter 7
Integrated Centers

Every chapter has specifically mentioned, and the friendly lion has subtly announced, the importance of integrating learning centers to include every possible discipline and as many activities as the imaginative teacher can create. The contents of this segment will clearly illustrate how to integrate centers fully to ensure the best learning environment possible in any given situation. All you have to do is use your eyes and put one of these sample plans in focus.

(All these centers were described earlier in the book for use with a specific subject area.)

Sounds We Know

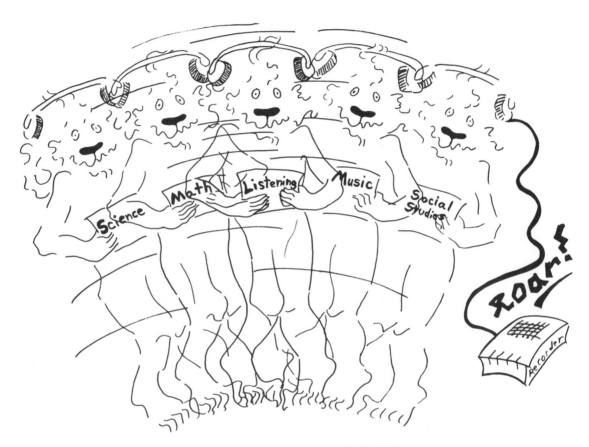

WHAT'S IT FOR?

To listen to and identify sounds on a tape recorder.

STUFF YOU'LL NEED

- ten to twelve pictures that depict the various sounds recorded on a tape
- cassette tape recorder
- prepared tape sounds of car, jet airplane, door shutting, dogs barking, and so on

HOW'S IT WORK?

Listening—Children play the tape and listen for a sound. When they recognize the sound, they find the picture that shows it and hold it up.

HOW'D THEY DO?

Except for the math activity, there is no paper check on the children's work in these centers. Observation is the best way to tell how the center is working. Is the tape recorder easy to use for the children? Does there need to be a limit to the number of children allowed in the center at the same time? Are the sounds too easily identified, or are they too hard? Do children have fun in these centers?

FIT'N IT IN

Math—Children listen for recorded claps. They count them, then circle that numeral on the appropriate row of their worksheet. If a number board is used, they put up the number they hear. Continue listening and recording the number of claps until the tape runs out. Have an answer sheet showing the correct order of numbers clapped so children can check their papers.

Music—One child at a time listens to a tape of rhythms played on a drum (with a pause after each rhythm) and tries to duplicate the rhythm he hears.

Science—Children play a tape of sounds animals make. As soon as they recognize the animal, they hold up its picture.

Social Studies—Children listen to a tape of sounds associated with community helpers—a police car or fire engine whistle, construction noises, and so on. They hold up the picture of the one they are hearing.

Nyms—Synonyms, Antonyms, and Homonyms

WHAT'S IT FOR?

To develop an understanding of the structure of words and their meanings.
To encourage creativity.
To provide fun activities.
To demonstrate a working knowledge of synonyms, antonyms, and homonyms.
To learn that many words can mean the same as other words.
To learn that many words can sound alike, yet have completely different meanings.
To recognize and use synonyms, antonyms, and homonyms in many content areas.
To use the dictionary to find meanings of words.
To enjoy creative writing by writing cinquains.

STUFF YOU'LL NEED

- dictionary
- construction paper
- poster paper or tagboard
- laminating paper or clear contact paper
- plywood, hinges (display board), or large cardboard
- cans
- Magic Markers
- tape
- stapler
- scissors
- folders
- books
- newspapers
- games
- grease pencil

HOW'S IT WORK?

1. Students begin work with "Surprise Package," completing activities on synonyms, antonyms, and homonyms (see page 33). Students choose activities relating to work in the content areas. Activities 2 through 9 are set up to be given directly to students.

2. Do you know the difference in each pair of words? Can you use each in a sentence? Look words up in the dictionary if necessary.
   weight, wait
   plain, plane
   lead, led
   weigh, way
   air, heir
   sun, son
   brake, break
   bare, bear
   Can you think of other pairs of words?

Homonyms

Box

3. Read each sentence, deciding which is the correct homonym to use. Underline with grease pencil. Then ask the teacher or a friend to check your work. The patchwork quilt was made (by, buy) my grandmother.
I (know, no) the definition of a right angle.
Will you please take the puppy (to, too, two) the veterinarian.

4. [Content area of science, unit on space travel]
Complete the activity by using synomyms to make your writing more colorful.
Man has always (dreamed _____) of reaching the moon. But first (powerful _____) rockets had to be developed. The astronauts had to be (well _____) trained for the (long _____) voyage . . .

5. [Content area of science, unit on space travel]
Write antonyms for each of these space words:
weightless
upward
horizontal
motion

6. [Content area of math, unit on addition]
Is "number" a synonym for "numeral"?
Write your answer using the grease
pencil.

———————————————————
———————————————————

Is "inverse operation" a synonym for
"subtraction"?

———————————————————
———————————————————

Can you think of a synonym for "set"?

———————————————————
———————————————————

Read this statement: 152 is another
name for fifteen 10's, two 1's.
Do the numbers mean the same? Do
synonyms mean the same or different?
Antonyms are words with opposite
meanings. What is the opposite of
these math words?
addition
subtraction
multiplication
division

7. [Content area of social science, unit on
cities]
Look at the picture of New York City.
Then write synonyms for these words:
large
great
crowded
awesome
busy

8. [Content area of social science, unit on
the United States]
Antonyms are words that mean the
opposite. Find words that mean the
opposite of the words in parentheses.
America is an (independent
———————————) country.
It is a land of (freedom
———————————).
The United States is a large (nation
———————————).

9. [Content area of social science, unit on
cities]
Have you ever written a cinquain? A
cinquain is a form of poetry made up
of only five lines and only twelve
words:
Line 1—title (one word or name)
Line 2—two words (describing title)
Line 3—three words (an action or verb)
Line 4—four words (a feeling about
Line 1)
Line 5—one word (a synonym for the
title)
Now are you ready to write your own
cinquain? New York has been
suggested as a title because we are
studying this city. Or you may want to
choose your own city.
New York

——————— ———————

——————— ——————— ———————

——————— ——————— ——————— ———————

———————

HOW'D THEY DO?

Teacher checks work in individual folders
as students complete activities.
Students work together and evaluate work
for each other.
Students rely on self-evaluation.

Look What's Cooking

WHAT'S IT FOR?

To develop understanding of prefixes and root words.

To demonstrate a working knowledge of prefixes and root words in various content areas.

To demonstrate skill in analyzing new words in terms of prefixes and Latin roots—before looking them up in the dictionary.

To learn that many words in the English language have Latin roots and prefixes.

To learn that knowing the meaning of only a few of the Latin roots helps one to know the meaning of many words.

To be able to recognize Latin roots in words taken from the various content areas.

To use a vocabulary of Latin words to unlock the meaning of many words.

To use the dictionary to see if words contain familiar prefixes or roots.

STUFF YOU'LL NEED

- display board
- envelopes
- Magic Markers
- scissors
- glue
- tape
- stapler
- boxes
- poster paper
- tagboard
- laminating film or clear contact paper
- grease pencil
- dictionary

HOW'S IT WORK?

Students begin with number 1 and complete each activity in sequence through number 8 to get the concept of prefixes and root words (these activities are presented on page 35). Numbers 9 through 15 provide for much practice in applying skills learned in numbers 1 through 8 and make application of knowledge in the various content areas.

1. Examine the definition of "prefix" and study common prefixes and their meanings.
2. Identify the prefix for each of several words and place in an envelope.
3. Make words with a prefix wheel.
4. Examine other prefixes and definitions.
5. Examine definitions of root words, and change root words by adding prefixes.
6. Play a root-word "fish" game.
7. Read the story given. Underline prefixes once and circle all root words.
8. Correct work in number 7 with answer key and put papers in envelopes.

9. [Content area of health, unit on disease]
A way to find meanings of new words is to see if words contain root words that you know. What do these words taken from the health textbook mean?
immune
immunize
immunity
immunization
infect
infection
disinfect
Use each in a sentence, orally. [Or someone can work with you]
How do the roots help you? Discuss with another student.

10. [Content area of health]
These words are in your text:
microscope
microorganism
What does the prefix "micro" mean?
What do the words mean?
Name other words with the prefix "micro".

11. [Content area of math, multiplication]
What new words can be made with "multiply"? Write your words below. Then compare your words with those on the back of the card.
What does the prefix "multi" mean? Look up the meaning in the dictionary. What new words can be made with "number" by adding prefixes or by changing the root? Check your words with the words on the back of the card.

12. [Content area of geography, unit on cities]
New words can be made by combining prefixes and root words. What is the meaning of the word "urban"?
Is the meaning of "urban" changed in these words? Why or why not? Discuss with another student.
urbanize
urbanization
suburb
suburban

13. [Content area of geography, unit on cities]
    Which would you be likely to find in urban areas? Check the correct words.
    tall buildings
    residential areas
    heavy traffic
    museums
    Name things likely to be found in suburbs.

14. [Content area of language arts]
    You can form new words by combining prefixes with roots.
    What new words are made when these prefixes and roots are combined?
    in (meaning *not*) + aud _____
    in (meaning *in*) + scrib _____
    re + vis _____
    inter + ject _____
    ex + tent _____

HOW'D THEY DO?

The teacher evaluates work completed by students.
Many activities are self-checking.
Students evaluate partners' work.

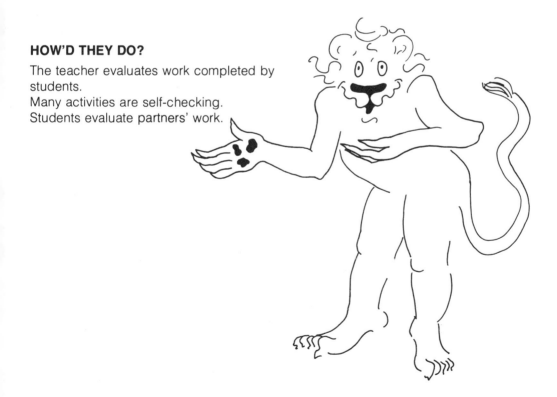

The Funny Farm

WHAT'S IT FOR?

To review and reinforce new vocabulary words on plant unit in science.

To utilize math skills in relation to unit on plants.

To use concepts about plants for creative writing.

STUFF YOU'LL NEED

- construction paper
- poster board
- markers
- tape
- display board or box
- mimeographed sheets
- plain paper
- ruler

HOW'S IT WORK?

Children may select which activity they begin with. No sequence is necessary.

1. *Leaf Fun*—Children take a mimeographed sheet of scrambled letters and arrange them correctly to spell "plant" words. *Integration Activity:* Children use their knowledge about plants to write or tell a meaningful dialogue between two trees.

2. *Fun forest*—Children pretend they are a redwood tree that is 269 years old. They write a short story describing events of their lifetime, including stages of their growth, geological changes they have seen, and technological and social changes they have seen. *Integration Activities:* (a) Determine how to tell the age of a tree. Bring in sections of tree trunks and determine the ages of the trees. (b) Make a scrapbook depicting all of the products of trees, such as paper and lumber.

3. *The Art Garden*—Make a seed collage. *Integration Activity:* Plant a seed. Keep a log of how the plant changes each day. Measure the plant each week. Determine how many inches the plant grows each week.

4. *Tool Shed*—Using plant flash cards and calendars, children figure out when vegetables will be ready.

5. *Word Jumble*—Students find and circle "plant" words in a jumble of letters.

HOW'D THEY DO?

Written papers are placed in a hand-in box for teacher review.
Logs are checked by teacher.
Teacher-pupil conferences are held.

Focus in on Math

WHAT'S IT FOR?

To integrate math concepts with other curriculum areas.

STUFF YOU'LL NEED

- display board
- games
- poster board
- string
- markers
- glue
- tape
- scissors
- tape recorder
- writing paper
- pencils
- crayons

HOW'S IT WORK?

Children may choose any activity to begin or may be directed to specific activities they need.

1. *Math Messages*—Children complete activities on basic combinations in addition, subtraction, multiplication, or division. *Integration Activities:* (a) Unscramble words related to the basic combinations, such as "addition," "subtraction," "multiplication," "division," and word names for the numerals. (Individual letters for spelling each word could be in separate envelopes, or the letters for each word could be written in incorrect order and the learner could write the correct spelling for each word.) (b) Choose a career and write or record reasons for a person who has that particular skill to know basic arithmetic. (c) Write or record reasons for an elementary student to know the basic arithmetic facts other than getting a passing grade in math.

2. *Square Up*—Puzzle pieces are fitted together to form a square. *Integration Activities:* (a) Other shapes could be made from fitting pieces of puzzles together. The child could choose any of the shapes and draw all of the places where this shape might be found, or the child could write or record the information or could role-play the many uses of a particular shape. (b) The child could make puzzles for others to work.

3. *Land on the Moon Game*—Basic combinations (any computational area) are used to go by steps to the moon. *Integration Activities:* (a) The child, using his scientific knowledge, writes, records, or illustrates an imaginary trip to the moon. (b) The child writes, records, or discusses the role of mathematics in taking a trip to the moon.

4. *Multiplication Football*—Children move down the football field by giving correct responses to basic multiplication facts. *Integration Activity:* One child role-plays a sports commentator by giving a play-by-play account of what is taking place on the football field.

HOW'D THEY DO?

Written work and illustrations are placed in a hand-in box for teacher comments. If possible, individual conferences are held as pupils complete activities, or pupils may sign up for conferences.

Japanese Jamboree

WHAT'S IT FOR?

To learn about Japan and Japanese customs.
To stimulate interest in study of Japan.

STUFF YOU'LL NEED

- travel guides for Japan
- study prints and pictures
- maps
- writing paper and pencil
- Japanese costumes (could be made or improvised)
- chopsticks
- Japanese currency (could be made)

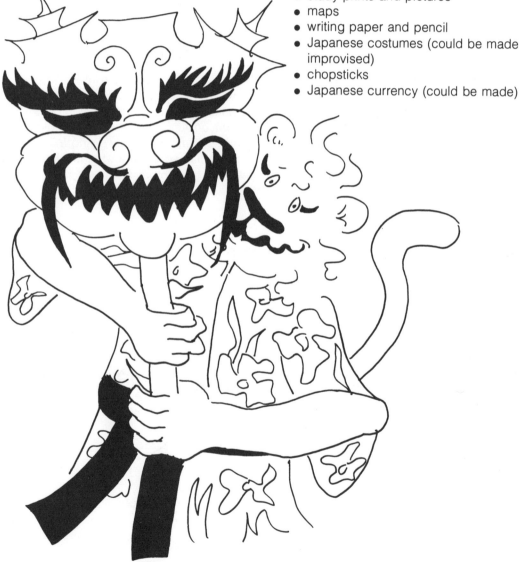

HOW'S IT WORK?

1. *Math*—Plan a Japanese tour for one week. Determine the cost of the flight, hotel, food, and so on. Determine the number of miles from the United States to Japan by air and the number of miles between major Japanese cities. Convert United States currency to Japanese currency and vice versa. Determine the difference in time.

2. *Language Arts*—Write a diary of daily events while taking an imaginary tour of Japan. Role-play a Japanese tour guide. Role-play news events of Japan. Write letters to classmates describing a major highlight of the tour. Write to a Japanese pen pal. Translate Japanese words into English and vice versa.

3. *Creative Arts*—Sing Japanese songs. Perform ceremonial dances and drama. Plan a Japanese meal and dress in costumes for serving the meal; use chopsticks. Do origami.

HOW'D THEY DO?

Diaries, letters, and tour planning could be shared with the whole class and turned into the teacher.

Teacher observation and pupil-teacher conferences should be utilized.

suggested readings

Berger, Evelyn, and Winters, Bonnie A. *Social Studies in the Open Classroom.* New York: Teachers College Press, 1973.

Carswell, Evelyn, and Roubinek, Darrell L. *Open Sesame . . . A Primer in Open Education.* Pacific Palisades, Calif.: Goodyear Publishing, 1974.

Collier, Mary Jo; Forte, Imogene; and MacKenzie, Joy. *Kids' Stuff, Nursery School and Kindergarten.* Nashville, Tenn.: Incentive Publications, 1969.

Cote, Bernard, and Gurske, Barbara. "Learning Center Guide," San Jose, Calif.: CTM, 1972.

Davidson, Tom; Fountain, Phyllis; and Grogan, Rachel. *Using Chart Racks, Easels, and Assorted Things To Hang Stuff On.* Carrollton, Ga.: The authors, 1974.

Davidson, Tom, and DeLong, Diane. "Are You Open," in Paula W. Smith and Verl M. Short (eds.), *A Point in Time . . . Readings In Early Childhood Education.* New York: MSS Information Corporation, 1973.

Dean, Joan. *Room to Learn: Working Space.* New York: Citation Press, 1973.

Dean, Joan. *Room to Learn: A Place to Paint.* New York: Citation Press, 1973.

Dean, Joan. *Room to Learn: Language Areas.* New York: Citation Press, 1973.

Forte, Imogene, and MacKenzie, Joy. *Nooks, Crannies and Corners . . . Learning Centers for Creative Classrooms.* Nashville, Tenn.: Incentive Publications, 1972.

Fountain, Phyllis, and Grogan, Rachel. "Learning Centers," in Paula W. Smith and Verl M. Short (eds.), *A Point in Time . . . Readings in Early Childhood Education.* New York: MSS Information Corporation, 1973.

Fountain, Phyllis; Grogan, Rachel; and Davidson, Tom. *Doors, Closets, Bookcases and Desks.* Carrollton Ga.: The authors, 1974.

Gingell, Lesley P. *The ABC's of the Open Classroom.* Homewood, Ill.: ETC Publications, 1973.

Godfrey, L. L. *Individualize with Learning Station Themes.* Menlo Park, Calif.: Individualized Books Publishing, 1973.

Grogan, Rachel; Fountain, Phyllis; and Davidson, Tom. *The Many Uses of Cardboard and Cardboard Boxes.* Carrollton, Ga.: The authors, 1974.

Howes, Virgil M. *Informal Teaching in the Open Classroom.* New York: Collier-Macmillan, 1974.

Kaplan, Sandra Nina. Kaplan, JoAnn Butom; Madsen, Sheila Kunishima; and Taylor, Bette K. *Change for Children.* Pacific Palisades, Calif.: Goodyear Publishing, 1973.

Kaplan, Sandra Nina; Kaplan, JoAnn Butom; Madsen, Sheila Kunishima; and Gould, Bette Taylor. *A Young Child Experiences.* Pacific Palisades, Calif.; Goodyear Publishing, 1975.

Lloyd, Dorothy M. *70 Activities for Classroom Learning.* Dansville, N.Y.: The Instructor Publications Company, 1974.

Lorton, Mary Barells. *Workjobs: Activity-Centered Learnings for Early Childhood Education.* Menlo Park, Calif.: Addison-Wesley, 1974.

Noar, Gertrude. *Individualized Instruction: Every Child a Winner.* New York: Wiley, 1972.

Nyguise, Ewald B., and Hawes, Gene R. *Open Education . . . A Sourcebook for Parents & Teachers.* New York: Bantam Books, 1972.

Schaffer, Frank. *Reading Activity Cards for Fun.* Palos Verdes, Calif.: The author, 1973.

Schaffer, Frank. *All About Me.* Palos Verdes, Calif.: The author, 1973.

Short, Verl M. "The Open Classroom," in Paula W. Smith and Verl M. Short (eds.), *A Point in Time . . . Readings in Early Childhood Education.* New York: MSS Information Corporation, 1973.

Stahl, Dona Dofod, and Arzalone, Patricia Murphy. *Individualized Teaching in Elementary Schools.* West Nyack, N.Y.: Parker Publishing, 1970.

Stephens, Lillian S. *The Teachers' Guide to Open Education.* Atlanta: Holt, Rinehart and Winston, 1974.

Sweeney, Connie; Johnson, Mary; and Bullard, Bobbie. *Centers Anyone?* Bloomington, Ind.: Phi Delta Kappa, 1974.

Taylor, Joe. *Organizing the Open Classroom—A Teachers' Guide to the Integrated Day.* New York: Shocken Books, 1972.

Voight, Ralph Claude. *Invitation to Learning.* Washington, D.C.: Acropolis, 1971.

Voight, Ralph Claude. *Invitation to Learning, 2.* Washington D.C.: Acropolis, 1975.

Wade, Priscilla,.and Short, Verl M. *Learning Centers for Everyone.* Carrollton, Ga.: Southeast Educators Services, 1975.

Waterman, Anita, and Pflum, John. *Open Education—For Me?* Washington, D.C.: Acropolis, 1974.

Waynant, L. F., and Wilson, R. M. *Learning Centers: A Guide for Effective Use.* Paoli, Pa.: The Instructo Corporation, 1973.